DYLAN THOMAS

Dylan Thomas

A literary study by

DEREK STANFORD

THE CITADEL PRESS
NEW YORK

FIRST PAPERBOUND EDITION 1964

PUBLISHED BY THE CITADEL PRESS
222 PARK AVENUE SOUTH, NEW YORK 3, N.Y.
COPYRIGHT 1954, © 1964 BY DEREK STANFORD
MANUFACTURED IN THE UNITED STATES OF AMERICA
LIBRARY OF CONGRESS CATALOG CARD NUMBER 64-19475

This revised edition contains a new section, entitled
"A Literary Post-Mortem."

CONTENTS

Introduction   I

Part I   *The Myth and the Man*   7

Part II *The Poems*   31

   18 Poems   31
   25 Poems   64
   The Map of Love   83
   Deaths and Entrances   90
   Last Poems   129
   Critics, Style and Value   144

Part III *Prose and Drama*   155

   Prose   155
   Drama   169

Part IV *A Literary Post-Mortem*   189

Selected Bibliography   207

List of First Lines   211

DYLAN THOMAS

Introduction

A WORD AS to the origin of this book and its plan of presentation.

Late-comer as I was to the poetry of Dylan Thomas, this present volume can make no claims to being the result of several years' study. Not till I was won to enthusiasm for some half a dozen of his poems, by a friend in 1949, could I say that the poet had meant much to me. Up to that time my casual objection to Thomas' verse had been the common one: that his meaning was too obscure and his style too obfuscated. To defend my hasty inquiry and retreat, I would tell myself that Coleridge, for his part, had observed that "To please me, a poem must be either music or sense ; if it is neither, I confess I cannot interest myself in it."

This retort was all very well for giving the go-by to some of the poet's more indefatigable and forward admirers, but did not quite satisfy my own questioning. I knew that the scriptures of the critics contained other texts to off-set this one; Goethe, for example, having written that "Excellent work is unfathomable, approach it as you will", and again, that "All lyrical work must, as a whole, be perfectly intelligible, but in some particulars a little unintelligible."

These two statements seemed to me to provide a more liberal ground of approach to poetry we describe as 'difficult' than Coleridge's cursory dismissal. It is true that by Goethe's term 'unfathomable' I understood 'that which we cannot exhaust, that which we cannot come to the bottom of' rather than 'that which rebuts our understanding'; but how could I be sure that I had come to the bottom of Thomas' poetry when I had hardly undertaken the first earnest steps in elucidation? Goethe's second maxim seemed even more pertinent. It posited that the bulk of a poem, as to the substance of its meaning, should be clear, but that certain incidents might remain dark or ambiguous. In other words, applying this maxim to Thomas, I had to ask myself the question, 'Is there a central meaning to his poetry; or, rather, is there a substantial meaning to be found in each of his separate poems however obscure the environment in which the meaning is situated?' Before I could reply to this I felt that any real judgement on Thomas' poetry must be suspended.

So desultory had been my reading of the poet that I had not discerned, till my friend virtually initiated me into some measure of appreciation of Thomas, that, quite outside the solution of this general problem, there existed a small number of his poems which called for little or no exegesis. To these I was rapidly 'converted'. Especially did I become an adherent of the last poem in the poet's volume *Deaths and Entrances*, the justly-famed *Fern Hill*. This gave to me a similar sort of excitement to that which my adolescence had found in Swinburne many years ago. There was a parallel lyricism in it, and something of the same plangency and pathos of sound and meaning. But whereas the pleasure I derived from Swinburne was now of a largely auditory order, limited to the music of his words, the pleasure I obtained from the poem *Fern Hill* seemed to me more composite and whole. Not only was I delighted by the movement and rhythm of the piece but I was also moved by the poem taken as a human statement. That is to say I discovered in it those imaginative reminders concerning the nature of human existence which justify us in speaking of a poem as offering a 'criticism of life'.

And so, for a number of years, the question I had propounded to myself regarding the body of Thomas' work remained shelved and unanswered. The repertoire of my appreciation of his poems was gradually widened, and slowly I assayed to read the mass of his verse. But still I continued detached in my opinion: I had not become engaged in his work with that closeness of application which finally leads to a reasoned judgment. Nor did I enter the struggle at close-quarters until after the poet's death.

Reading the report of the poet's illness—his loss of consciousness in New York—I became aware that the fate of some rare element was hanging in the balance. The announcement of his death brought home to me an intimation of what had been extinguished. The knowledge of his decease, and the disappearance of his person from the uninspired scenes in which we move, was like the theft of a force of nature which, in its lustre, we had taken for granted. To distinguish a little, but not I hope too finely, I felt that not only had English poetry endured a desolating loss, but that the English poetic imagination had itself suffered a disaster. What I imply by this division is, that, apart from the enrichment of English verse by his own contribution, a poet sometimes augments our consciousness of poetry by his personality, his talk, and mode of living. Swinburne and Rimbaud were of this class of poets; and in our own day, in these circumspect islands, Thomas provided a superb illustration.

I remember how, the day following his death, my mind was haunted by lines from his poems. The weather was windy, cold, and bright; and the shapes of things in the late autumn sunshine seemed to call out for interpretation, for endorsement, in the poet's individual style. This direct impingement of another's vision upon my own way of seeing things continued for a course of days.

If, so far, I have been unduly personal, I must ask the reader to excuse me, with the assurance that—this Introduction over—I shall not be intruding much again. My reason for discoursing so upon my own reactions has been to present, honestly, my position in relation to the poet. Now that I come to write my book, I hope that the slow-ish process I made in reading him is a sort of credential for a work which sets out to explain his meaning, on the assumption that the meaning is not easy.

The method I propose in dealing with the poet's verse is that of a conducted tour of the poems. My first intention will be to discover what the poem is about, and, next, what it says about the subject it deals with. In the course of doing this, I shall pass incidental value-judgments on the worth of the poem as poetry; but my chief concern will be with the meaning. A general chapter on Thomas' poetry will attempt to evaluate his verse; but the main purpose of the book is to offer a commentary. My study of Thomas' verse will not deal fully with all his poems. Where I can make neither head nor tail of a poem, as to meaning or style, I shall say so, briefly, giving my reasons. The rejections I make and the reasons I advance, I shall consider personal and provisional: it is possible that some other sensibility may find meaningful what I find pointless.

On the whole I shall try to subdue my mind to the poet's work. In former works of criticism, my reviewers have sometimes remarked a too great tendency to generalisation. This, I do not think, will be met with here. At the same time, of course, I write from a viewpoint, though this is not the same as writing for a Cause. To substantiate my view-point, my frame of vision, I propose to make use of two hypotheses, which the reader may find suggestive or helpful. To these assumptions I shall not ask the reader's entire intellectual assent. I shall merely ask him to consider the poetry in the light of their assumptive truths. If he finds that these ideas (which I introduce in the nature of guides or analogies) impede his appreciation of the poems, he has my encouragement to dismiss them; for, above all, with this poet, I believe the text to be the thing.

I would like my book to be regarded as a sort of companion volume to the poet's *Collected Poems*, and for the two to be read in conjunction My book is not one of those critical works which the reader may choose to study in place of the original Its purpose has been to serve the poet The text which I have used and quoted is that of the *Collected Poems*.

And now, as touching what I shall omit as outside the unity intended in this work My chief omission will be in anything like a complete assessment of the influence of other poets upon Thomas. Henry Treece, in his book on the poet, has pursued such a line of inquiry; his remarks on Thomas' debt to Hopkins and Welsh verse-forms being particularly interesting.[1] On the other hand, I shall have something to say about the poet's inheritance of certain aspects of the Celtic mind.

Neither shall I attempt to trace Thomas' influence upon his contemporaries. This, again, has been discharged by Henry Treece, especially the story of the relationship between the poet and the Apocalyptic Movement, and the position which both of them took up to Surrealism.

I should like to take this opportunity of thanking Mr. Treece, who generously assured me that there was plenty of room for my book.

I should also like to recognise the assistance I have had in writing my book from the work of previous critics of Thomas. My thanks are principally due to

---

[1] Though regarded with strong suspicion, I gather, by many Welsh-speaking poets and critics.

Francis Scarfe, for his essay on the poet in his book *Auden and After* (1942); to the American critic, Marshall Stearns, for his pamphlet *Unsex the Skeleton : Notes on the Poetry of Dylan Thomas* (1944); and to Linden Huddlestone, for his study *An Approach to Dylan Thomas* in *Penguin New Writing*.

I have prefaced my study of Thomas' poems with a biographical chapter. This is not meant to offer a factual and 'authoritative' account of the poet's life, but rather to serve as an atmospheric 'lead-in' to his poetry. Its purpose is to suggest to the reader the man behind the poetry, and to relate the one to the other. This impressionistic sketch I have assembled from various sources: from the reports of those who knew him, either intimately or in passing; from random remarks of the poet himself; and, lastly, from his own recollections of his youth in *Portrait of the Artist as a Young Dog*. In this synthesis I have not guarded against the entry of mythical fragments, since any man who is a poet is perhaps as much a myth as a person.

My book concludes with two chapters on Thomas' prose and dramatic writings.

PART ONE

The Myth and the Man

I

DYLAN MARLAIS THOMAS was born in the October of 1914 at Swansea and died in the November of
1953 in New York. His life was short: a mere thirty-
nine years, but leaves us with no impression of time
wasted. "I shall be dead within two years", he told
R. B. Marriott[1] in 1935, when he was only twenty-one,
"drinking, exploring, going to the devil."[2] From the
first, he possessed—or affected to possess—a premo-
nition of his allotted span, and from the first he seemed
to think that his future would allow him no procrasti-
nation. It was necessary for him to decide what sort of
figure he was to be; and at an age when most children
leave all decisions to parents and teachers, Thomas had
resolved the matter for himself: his *persona* was fixed—
he was to be a poet.

This resolution he carried out with a singleness of
purpose which would have been exceptional at all
times, and was doubly so in our own 'utility' epoch.
The transition from vocation to career, which most
poets make as the years waylay them, was a declension
he utterly rejected. His integrity here was adamant.

From the ingenious sins of compromise Thomas was
saved both by his vices and his virtues. If we consider,

---

[1] *Adam* no. 238 (1953).
[2] *ibid.* R. B. Marriott's words.

7

for example, his obstinancy and intransigence—his refusal to accord to convention the smallest grain of Chinese politeness—and relate this occasional ungraciousness to his dedicated task, we shall find it hard to separate from a high ideal of functional purity. He had decided to be a poet, and was determined that life should not succeed in making him anything else. Neither would he let it over-lay his chosen role, nor subtly corrupt, deflect, or prostitute it.

I have spoken of Thomas' choice in this matter—of his conscious self-appointment to the office of poet—and feel my words call for qualification. We all know Horace's tag about the poet being born, not made; and remember how Shelley remarked that no man, by taking thought, can say to himself "I will be a poet". But once given this gift at birth, a man can take thought as to how he shall use it. Most of those who feel poetic stirrings, together with some earnest of a talent in verse, depart from the pure and single idea of acting the poet, and nothing but the poet, any time between their twenties and their thirties. The first descent is usually marked when they begin to think of themselves as 'poet and critic'; and from this they pass to a lower level whereon they justify their dissipated powers by calling themselves 'men of letters'. These practical, convenient, and profitable off-shoots of the poetic gift, Thomas refused to cultivate in any save a poetic spirit. If he wrote for broadcasting, he did not believe that such sort of work excused him from aiming at standards of perfection. Whatever he committed, in verse or in prose, was executed consciously: by a poet, observant of the standards of a poet, and not as so much journalistic script. Like Cardinal Newman, he could claim: "Every thought I think is thought, and every word I write is writing."

By this, I do not mean that his literary ideal kept him on a pedestal or from gaily unbending. In writing, he recognised many registers besides that of 'the grand style'; and the comic, the satiric, and the mischievous were often employed by him. But whether it was a piece of verse, rhapsodic and exultant in tone, or a skittish passage of parody that Thomas was composing, one consideration prevailed: platitude, flatness, and cliché were forbidden. The words had to be personal, arranged in an order not exhibited before.

But if the poetry of 'the man of letters' loses through its author's indiscriminate composition, the poet himself may be the gainer in terms of general civility. In coming to associate poetry with the different arts and sciences—with other airs and graces of 'the good life'— he becomes a more civilised person. His manners, taste, and understanding tend to become developed and improved. It may be argued that this process is largely a superficial one, and that it chiefly consists in disguising "the dog beneath the skin", which stays untouched by such amelioration. This must be admitted; yet it still remains that the rollers of social intercourse work the more smoothly for it. Life, after all, as Matthew Arnold stated, is predominantly a matter of conduct and only secondarily a concern of art. The most original poets, solely, through what they bequeath us, appear justified in ignoring or reversing these proportions.

That Thomas ignored them was apparent. "The least literary of men",[3] John Davenport called him; and this lack of cultural interests was the least result of his antinomianism. That when on a visit to Italy, "he preferred the ironworkers of Elba to the literary cliques of Florence or Rome, and even went so far on one occasion to lock himself in a cupboard to avoid the famous representative of one coterie"[4] need not be

[3] *Dylan Thomas*, an essay in *The Twentieth Century* (Dec. 1953).
[4] *ibid*. In a letter to a friend, the poet, when in Italy, wrote "We have got to know lots of the young intellectuals of Florence, and a damp lot they are. . . . Do you know anybody in Florence nice to have a drink with?"

accounted against him; but his detestation of formality and the insistent anarchy of his nature could take more extreme forms than this. Derek Patmore has told us how, whilst staying in Florence, the poet "horrified his Italian hosts by suddenly tearing down the curtains in one of the rooms in his villa";[5] and when he was living in South Leigh, a small hamlet near Witney ("blanketty Witney" was how he described it), just outside of Oxford, Suzanne Roussillat has described how "he used to spend many merry evenings there in the company of a few friends, generally of Celtic origin; to the academic entertainments of the time-honoured University town, they preferred a stroll at night in the picturesque lanes of the old city, going from pub to pub, never so happy when their unusual garb, or crude language, scandalised their neighbours who knew how to drink beer and remain formal."[6]

Here it becomes necessary to distinguish between what was natural and what was assumed in this attitude of the poet. His dislike of formal manners and occasions was instinctive and sincere: his reactions against them sometimes exaggerated, sometimes the result of the role which he had appropriated to himself. This role is best defined in his own language as "The Provincial Rush, or the Up-Rimbaud-and-At-Em approach."[7] It consisted of an ultra-bohemianism, often aggressive in its showing, and not perhaps without its calculating side. If one accepted it, or revealed oneself amenable, the poet responded with a courtesy which, though possibly dreamy, was exquisite. Myself, I remember meeting him at a party towards the end of the war. He was certainly intoxicated (as I was too, on that occasion), and along with some friends was

---

[5] *Adam* no. 238 (1953).
[6] *ibid.*
[7] *How to be a Poet* (2) an article in *Circus*, no. 2 May (1950).

treading out the measure of a slow impromptu circular dance. The dancers all faced inwards; and, standing on the periphery, I greeted him by name as his shuffling figure came revolving round. Hearing himself called, he turned to face me, and, with a fine old-world gesture, bowed and said "Good evening, sir". I had never spoken to the poet before, and was taken by his grave natural politeness. Unprovoked, and in an atmosphere which he felt congenial to him, I think his inborn courtesy was unfailing; but if ever he was challenged, or sensed himself subsisting in a spirit of middle-class decorum, his response was apt to be unfavourable.

Besides the truculence he revealed when his values seemed to be questioned, he could sometimes appear discourteous through an excess of shyness, though unmotivated by active ill-will. In the following account by Rosalind Wade of her early memories of the poet, both of these factors are clearly present. "He seemed to me," writes Miss Wade, "exceedingly small but it may have been the hunched way he had of sitting. He was scowling and it was obvious that he resented my presence. Although I was writing psychological novels about people whom the poets usually called 'bourgeois' I had become a close friend of the two Davids[8] and George Barker but I never felt that Dylan was ready to extend the slightest friendship, far less surface courtesy. Moreover, I was not instantly attracted to him: he was so *dirty*, nails, rain-coat, tangled curly hair. When I read recently that his father was a Grammar School Master I was amazed, for I had thought that the family must be without resources. Needless to say David Archer had the highest possible opinion of Dylan and certainly eccentric dress and absence of social graces never worried *him*, although

[8] David Archer, part-owner of the Parton Bookshop and Press, and David Gascoyne, one of the young poets published by David Archer.

he himself had a particular charm of manner, as had
David G. and George B. . . . I do not seem to have
many intermediate pictures in my memory of making
further acquaintance with Dylan, but must jump to
an occasion, some weeks or months later, when my
sister and I were spending the early part of the evening
at the Cafe Royal—(the old-style C.R. with the red-
haired Haidee leading her delectable little orchestra)
drinking beer on the marble-topped tables and
watching the diners in company with David Gascoyne and Dylan. We, my sister, David and I were to
go on afterwards to an evening party given by Joseph
Bard (critic, lecturer, writer, on the Council of the
R.S.L., and his wife Eileen Agar, the Surrealist
painter). I suggested taking Dylan. To my surprise,
he agreed to come, and I can remember the guests, all
in evening dress, sitting about on the low modern
shaped chairs in that carefully lit, predominantly white
drawing-room which had been the scene of so many
brilliant gatherings. Joseph welcomed Dylan en-
thusiastically, for he and Eileen had already admired
David Gascoyne's work. Since the room was already
rather crowded, some of us sat on cushions on the
floor—and I can see Dylan still, in my mind's eye—
seated cross-legged on a small *pouffe*—red-faced with
resentment or embarrassment, or both—resembling a
malignant gnome.

"On that occasion he wore, I cannot imagine why,
a very grubby green jersey of the kind supplied to
Wolf Cubs and his nails were certainly blacker than
ever, doubtless the grime of London and a life in extremely straitened circumstances had left their mark!
I do not know whether in fact the tasteful luxurious
surroundings and the well-dressed guests had the elementary psychological reaction of inducing the desire
to shock, rather as a certain type of child will scribble
on a clean wall. At any rate, whatever the reason, the

sight of the placid guests, relaxed and benign after
a good dinner, roused in him emotions of intense
hostility. He attacked everything and everybody,
interlarding his comments with any and every swear
word. If he had hoped to disrupt the atmosphere of
the party he was disappointed. I can remember Sir
William Crawford, not really aware of the disturbance,
lying back luxuriously, in a long chair—it was left to
Mrs. Ashley Havinden . . . to take the full blast of
Dylan's ire. But nothing he said embarrassed her. She
gave him as good as she got, as the saying is, querying
his statements, gently teasing him, laughing good-
humouredly at his blasphemies and begging him to
be more cheerful and to grow up. Dylan became more
and more morose and denunciatory, while our hosts
moved graciously about the room replenishing our
glasses. None of us were sticklers for formality, yet
next morning I felt a slight uneasiness about Dylan's
performance and telephoned Joseph to say so. He
expressed the greatest surprise at my concern. 'But we
were delighted,' he assured me. 'I hope Dylan will
come again.' "

These reminiscences of Miss Wade date back to
1934, when Thomas was a fledgling poet of twenty.
In 1946, Miss Wade met him again "at a literary dinner,
whither he was brought, under protest apparently, by
a party of admiring friends. He was unable to 'bear'
the preliminary social session, and went out to get a
drink. I feel certain that this horror of formality and
small talk was an utterly genuine reaction. Finally he
reappeared and sat through the meal, throwing pellets
of bread at the other diners. But when the 'talk'
began it was good to see his boredom and indifference
drop like a mask from his face, as he listened atten-
tively to every word and afterwards congratulated the
speaker with spontaneous enthusiasm. It was in this
mood that he delivered commentaries and broadcasts,

once the crust of resentment and seeming rudeness had been broken through. It is a matter of regret to me, that I personally had no success in breaking through it myself. I was in truth a little afraid of him."

Mood played a large part, I think, in the impression the poet created. "The highest wisdom in the world is happiness—that is the impact his personality left upon me," writes Mr. B. P. Rees of Swansea, who met him about a year before his death. The occasion was a poetry reading. "It was something quite informal and held at the late Lady Stepney's home. . . . I was introduced to him by the hostess before the reading: he was drinking—as if priming himself up for an ordeal but he was very charming and natural and what surprised me—having known lesser men and their inflated views of themselves—utterly without side. When, after the reading, we had a short chat over the coffee and sandwiches I suggested his learning Greek and translating Homer for us—I thought it might be good for him and for us—but no it would be too much for him—said so disarmingly as to make one feel it didn't really matter after all."

From his school-days there had been those who took his peculiarities and his pose for granted. At Swansea Grammar School, where his father taught English, his eccentricity seems to have been accepted. Wynford Vaughan Thomas tells us[9] how the poet met his head-master, one morning, on his way out of the playground; and was asked by the latter where he was going. Thomas replied that he was "going to take a few hours off". "Well, don't get caught," advised the head-master—a wise and ironic gentleman! Many a time, while at school, he was told that he must work harder; to which his invariable reply was, that he was going to write poetry. This, he presumed, was suffi-cient explanation.

[9] B.B.C. Home Service broadcast.

Thomas' early submission of himself to what Patrice de la Tour du Pin calls "the dedicated life of poetry" was doubtless a powerful stimulant to his growth. But while such a discipline gave him direction, it is possible to believe that it concentrated his faculties too narrowly. That must remain a debateable question; but what, I think, is more apparent is, that the accompanying role which Thomas decided on—the hell-raker, Ishmaelite, Rimbaud figure—was not without a number of draw-backs. The roaring life of one who is a law to himself may help to release in the young poet qualities too often inhibited; but the continuance of such a mode of living may prove a factor impeding development, when not making for disintegration. In a sense, Thomas was growing out of this phase; but that he was still partly under its influence is shown by what the poet told Harvey Breit[10] in 1950: "I should be what I was . . . twenty years ago. . . . Then I was arrogant and lost. Now I am humble and found. I prefer the other."

This somewhat fixated choice was also responsible for the cult of a too protracted sensationalism. Writing to the poet Alec Craig, about a celebration on the previous evening, Thomas gave his verdict: "It was a wonderful party, Alec, plenty to eat, plenty to drink, everybody made love to everybody else, and there was *real* fighting."[11] The poet often spoke with his tongue in his cheek, and the italics here suggest a conscious hyperbole. Yet, even so, an element of adolescent excitement-worship had its place in Thomas. Following one evening of heavy drinking, he told a friend who had been with him: "You remember that blonde who was drowning in her sherry. She killed herself last night after we left her." This desire to be 'in at the death' could make the poet sound callous. In fact,

[10] *Talk with D. Thomas* (*New York Times Book Review* May 14, 1950).
[11] *Dylan Thomas* by Alec Craig (*Plan*, vol. 2, no. 12, Dec. 1953).

he was a deeply compassionate man, with a great sympathy for the down-trodden. W. W. Rodgers has beautifully spoken of his tender responsiveness: "As water knows the lie of the land and birds smell the direction of the wind, Dylan would always take in what was your position any morning or night."[12]

Too often in their attention to the poet's self-generated myth, people would forget the man behind the legend: as modest, simple, affectionate, and tolerant as his bardic *alter-ego* was .arrogant and incorrigible. The poet Hugo Manning kept sight of them both, recording his evidence to both phenomena. In August of 1947 *The New Statesman* held a competition, the subject of which was to be some eminent person's nativity celebrated in a copy of verses. Hugo Manning, with his eye to the legendary figure of the poet, contributed the winning entry:

> Now bird-beast and song and making God in bed,
> Illumine like a nimbus your apocalyptic head,
> Ninety-one years on your journey to heaven.
> Enough nectar there was to excite and leaven
> The sullen art flowering on spindrift pages:
> Your burning song, far from ivory stages.
> "O worms, however, must still be fed," warn angels
> now as well as sages.
> "Not even poets can avoid saying their final prayers
> Ere drinking liquor in hell or reciting verse upstairs."

He likewise recalled the man behind the poet. "People will write and speak about Dylan Thomas' verse for a long time," he wrote, "but let us remember that he was also an artist in his friendliness. It was the rare friendliness which seems to belong to those who retain a childlike simplicity and wonder and who are unafraid of being hurt by living. . . . Dylan Thomas achieved what few writers could do in a single generation, but the inherent man or child in him retained

[12] B.B.C. Home Service broadcast.

its human flexibility and freshness. This in itself was a superb achievement."[13]

II

In his book of early sketches *Portrait of the Artist as a Young Dog*, we see Thomas laying the foundations of his myth. But, along with these snap-shot impressions of a born scally-wag, from the time of his first year at grammar-school to his short spell as a cub reporter, another glimpse of him is given—a half-pastoral provincial figure passionately in love with the circumstances of his local environment. This latter image, with its regional pieties, instinctive though hardly venerating, has other implications than the Rimbaud *persona*—the super-man type, which belongs nowhere but takes all the world for its stage.

In his description of his uncle's farm,[14] this intense sense of fidelity to place—of being a part of a whole— is present:

"The ramshackle outhouses had tumbling, rotten roofs, jagged holes in their sides, broken shutters, and peeling white-wash; rusty screws ripped out from the dangling, crooked boards; the lean cat of the night before sat snugly between the splintered jaws of bottles, cleaning its face, on the tip of the rubbish pile that rose triangular and smelling sweet and strong to the level of the riddled cart-house roof. There was nowhere like the farm-yard in all the slapdash county, nowhere so poor and grand and dirty as that square of mud and rubbish and bad wood and falling stone, where a bucketful of old and bedraggled hens scratched and laid small eggs. "

These confessions of natural affinity probably tell us as much about Thomas, as do the passages which set forth a portrait of a 'bad boy' in the making.

For example, the young school-boy poet (there are several actual school-day poems in the story called

<hr />

[13] *Adam* no. 238 (1953).
[14] In a story in the *Portrait* entitled *The Peaches*.

The Fight) paints himself as an inquisitive smut-hunting liar; but only the frankness in speaking of these traits, and not the traits themselves, is unusual:

> "Mrs. Bevan . . . began to eat. She was grey-haired and grey-faced. Perhaps she was grey all over. I tried to undress her, but my mind grew frightened when it came to her short flannel petticoat and navy bloomers to the knees. I couldn't even dare unbutton her tall boots to see how grey her legs were. She looked up from her plate and gave me a wicked smile.
>
> " Blushing, I turned to answer Mr. Jenkyn, who was asking me how old I was. I told him, but added one year."

There is so much authenticity here that the reader who retains only a trace of 'Little-Lord-Fauntleroy' idealism may fail to recognise the characterisation of a growing boy's behaviour. The 'naughtiness' depicted in these incidents is hardly one stage advanced on that of the lad of six or seven, soiling himself by playing on the coal-heap, and shouting out to his mother's maid, "You'd better come soon. . . . I'm dirty as Christ knows what!"[15]

The wild boy to be—the adult 'roaring boy'—makes no true appearance in these pages; though there are hints and indications of the image which time was to develop. In *Where Tawe Flows* we hear of "Young Mr. Thomas [who] was at the moment without employment, but it was understood that he would soon be leaving for London to make a career in Chelsea as a free-lance journalist; he was penniless, and hoped, in a vague way, to live on women." The future apostle of Bacchus is suggested by the figure of the young poet drinking in a Swansea pub. How lovingly the beer is described:

> "I leant against the bar, between an alderman and a solicitor, drinking bitter . . . . . I liked the taste of the beer, its live,

[15] *Patricia, Edith, and Arnold.*

white lather, its brass-bright depths, the sudden world through the wet brown walls of the glass, the tilted rush to the lips and the slow swallowing down to the lapping belly, the salt on the tongue, the foam at the corners."[16]

But there is little of that violent hedonism, which Thomas was to take as his creed, in the small adventures of the *Portrait*. In the last sketch *One Warm Saturday*, he seems eventually to have discovered the milieu and company for which he was seeking:

> "Mrs. Franklin raised her empty glass in a gloved hand and shook it like it a bell. 'Men are deceivers ever,' she said. 'And a drop of mother's ruin right around.'
> 'Especially Mr. Franklin,' said the barmaid.
> 'But there's a lot in what the preacher says, mind,' Mrs. Frankling said, 'about the carrying on. If you go for a constitutional after stop-tap along the sands you might as well be in Sodom and Gomorrah.'
> 'The blonde girl laughed. 'Hark to Mrs. Grundy! I see her with a black man last Wednesday, round by the museum."

But even these hopeful contacts result in nothing, and the evening comes to an abortive end.

The point is, that the *Portrait* conducts us only as far as Thomas' departure for London. Now it might be argued that the real flowering of the poet's dionysian *alter-ego* took place after what Sir Max Beerbohm describes as "the great apocalyptic moment of initiation into the fabulous metropolis"; that it was, in fact, something which strategy demanded—Thomas' designed reaction to his removal from Wales. Certainly he had no true liking for the capital; but London was essential to him, if he was to make his name with least delay. He decided to use it as a spring-board: to leap from its plank and take a soaring dive.

Nobody could ever accuse Thomas of favourably arranging his features before the public: the *Portrait* offers no plea in self-defence; and because of this

[16] *Old Garbo.*

absence of apologetics, I think it is important to record the only approbatory remark that Thomas has left about himself in these pages. It is so quietly, so reticently, inserted that it is easy for it to be passed over. It occurs in the story *Where Tawe Flows*, and shows us the "young Mr. Thomas" covering up a thoughtless word by another that might have hurt a mutual friend:

> " 'Why don't they have serials on matchboxes? You'd buy the shop up to see what Daphne did next,' Mr. Humphries said.
> He stopped and looked round in embarrassment at the faces of his friends. Daphne was the name of the grass widow in Manselton for whom Mr. Roberts had lost both his reputation and his position in the brewery. He had been in the habit of delivering bottles to her house, free of charge, and he had bought her a cocktail cabinet and given her a hundred pounds and his mother's rings. In return, she had held large parties and never invited him. Only Mr. Thomas had noticed the name, and he was saying: 'No, Mr. Humphries, on toilet rolls would be best.' "

It is only a little moment; but in its bashful testimony to the poet's kindness of heart and considerate sensibility, there is something pathetic. It is almost as if Thomas felt himself under compulsion to blacken his own name, and humbly hesitated to include anything, however small, to his credit.

III

"Men of humour," remarked Coleridge, "are always in some degree men of genius; wits are rarely so." Thomas' sense of the risible depended more on humour than on wit, though he did not lack the power of keen retort.

Strangely enough, his gift of humour served both for his self-expression and for his parody of others. Besides being a deft mimic, he relished literary travesty. "Some time in 1941 or early 1942," writes Mr. D. J. Ritchie, "Dylan Thomas attended a meeting of Oxford University English Club at which he read some parodies of contemporary poets. Certainly Auden and Spender—also I think Eliot and Macneice and Day Lewis. As far as I know these have not been published, and, if I remember rightly, nor do I know whether they could be!"

The snatches of parody that appeared in Thomas' essay *How to be a Poet* are shorter and less reprehensible than those which Mr. Ritchie enjoyed having heard; but, in their compact cameo-fashion, are scandalous and exquisite enough:

"If this were the 'twenties, Cedric's first book of poems, published while he was still an undergraduate, might be called 'Asps and Lutes'. It would be nostalgic for a world that never was. It would be world-weary. (He once saw the world, out of a train carriage window: it looked unreal.) It would be a carefully garish mixture, a cunningly evocative pudding full of plums pulled from the Sitwells and Sacheverell other people, a mildly cacophonous hothouse of exotic horticultural and comi-erotic bric-a-brac, from which I extract these typical lines:

> A cornucopia of phalluses
> Cascade on the vermillion palaces
> In arabesques and syrup rigadoons;
> Quince-breasted Circes of the zenanas
> Do catch this rain of cherry-wigged bananas
> And saraband beneath the raspberry moons.

"After a tiff with the University authorities he vanishes into the Key of Blue[17]—a made man.

"If it were in the 'thirties, the title of his book might well be 'Pharos, I warn,' and would consist of one or two kinds of verse. Either it would be made of long, lax, lackadaisical rhythms, dying falls, and images of social awareness:

[17] A reference to John Addington Symonds' book of that name; a volume of topographical and cultural studies, containing one or two pieces not without aesthetic homosexual significance.

> After the incessant means-test
>   of the conspiratorial winter
> Scrutinising the tragic history of each robbed branch,
> Look! the triumphant burgeoning! spring gay
>   as a workers' procession
> To the newly-opened gymnasium!
> Look! the full employment of the blossoms!

"Or it would be daringly full of slang and street phrases, snippets of song hits, Kipling jingles, kippered blues:

> We're sitting pretty
> In the appalling city—
> I know where we're going but I
>   don't know where from—
> Take it from me, boy,
> You're my cup-of-tea-boy,
> We're sitting on a big black bomb.

The prose comment which follows this delightfully, maliciously, 'blows the gaff' on the Public-School Socialism of the 'thirties with a foot in each of the two opposing worlds:

> "Social awareness! That was the motto. He would talk over coffee—. . . of spending the long vacation in 'somewhere *really* alive. I mean, but really. Like the Rhondda Valley or something. I mean, I know I'll really feel *oriented* there. I mean, one's so stagnant here. Books, books. It's people that count. I mean, one's got to know the miners.' And he spends the long vacation with Reggie, in Bonn. A volume of politico-travel chat follows, the promise of which is amply fulfilled when, years later, he turns up as Literary Secretary of I.A.C.T.—(International Arts Council Tomorrow)."

Daniel Jones, a boyhood friend of the poet, has described how, in their games together, Thomas and he had "word-obsessions: Everything at one time was 'little' or 'white'; and sometimes an adjective became irresistibly funny in almost any connection: 'innumerable bananas', 'wilful mocassin', 'a certain Mrs.

Prothero.' "[18] Years later, in a broadcast,[19] one of these capriciously captivating adjectives proved how well its selection had been justified. A crowd of rowdy drinking men are remarking on the antics of a drunken comrade:

"Look at Will Sentry, he's proper snobbled."
"Look at his wilful feet."

In his impromptu utterance, Thomas was vitally humorous. He could laugh at himself unmercifully, as well as mocking at the affectations of another. Drinking, one evening, in a truculent mood, he turned to an acquaintance in the bar. "I think I'll be going out to find C——. I'll make him put 'em up," he muttered, brandishing his fists. Whereupon the poet disappeared, to return not more than a few moments later, looking a deal less truculent. "Well," the acquaintance greeted him, "I though you were going to make him put 'em up." "I was, you know," replied the poet, "but he put them up first."[20]

As he grew older, Thomas developed something of Silenus' abdominal girth. Pushing his way, with portly belly, into a company of young men and women discussing what war-work they were going to do, the poet replied that—for himself—he was going "to volunteer as a tank."

Nothing amused Thomas more than the literary pose of 'high seriousness' Seeing a certain young writer holding himself aloof from the throng, with an air of attentive religious gloom, at a distinguished artistic *soirèe*, he answered—when asked who the young man was—"Oh, he's not a bad chap, really. Thinks he's God, but he's really quite nice."

Along with this flair for teasing and exposing, there

[18] *Encounter* no. 4 (Jan. 1954).
[19] *A Story* (published in *The Listener*, Sept. 17, 1953).
[20] Told me by Mr. Anthony Lincoln.

went a liking for speaking of things in terms of their lowest common denominator. This could be galling to the pretentious; and at one British Council party he insisted on referring to the coffee-cups and wine-glasses as being "lovely mugs".

IV

In the *Portrait of the Artist as a Young Dog*, there is one passage,[21] particularly, which reveals the Cymric or Celtic spirit in Thomas. Its essence consists of what we may term a familiarity with the divine, and its method of sudden surprising contrast.

Gwilym, the young poet's cousin, who is studying for the ministry, practices preaching in his father's barn:

> 'O God, Thou are everywhere all the time, in the dew of the morning, in the frost of the evening, in the field and the town, in the preacher and the sinner, in the sparrow and the big buzzard. Thou canst see everything, right down deep in our hearts; ... Thou canst see everything we do, in the night and day, in the day and the night, everything, everything; Thou canst see all the time. O God, mun, you're like a bloody cat.'

Not to accept the sincerity of this unanticipated descent would be to miss the racial element here. It is a peculiarly Welsh property, though not without a likeness to the Irish in such matters. In the poem ascribed to St. Bridget, for instance, generally referred to as *The Heavenly Banquet*, there is the same audacious meeting of the earthly and the heavenly, though in a more diffused manner:

> I would like to have the men of Heaven
> In my own house
> With vats of good cheer
> Laid out before them.

[21] *The Peaches.*

I would like them to be cheerful
In their drinking
I would like to have Jesus, too,
Here amongst them.

I would like to have a great lake of beer
For the King of Kings.
I'd love to be watching the family of heaven
Drinking it through all eternity.

Writing to Stephen Spender (December 9, 1952), Thomas confessed: "I'm not influenced by Welsh bardic poetry. I can't read Welsh."[22] The realisation of this truth, among critics who formerly looked to Welsh verse for an explanation of the poet's technique, may well lead to a further error—the denial of most Welsh characteristics as having a place in determining the nature of the poet.

Individual as Thomas' genius was, it gains in lucidity if we understand it in terms of the qualities of his own race. "For beauty and amorousness, the Gaedhils [the Gaels]", runs an old self-complimentary Irish verse; and 'beauty' and 'amorousness' do strongly inform and decide the spirit of Thomas' poetry.

To read Matthew Arnold's lectures on *The Study of Celtic Literature*, together with Ernest Renan's *Poetry of the Celtic Races*, is to encounter phrase after phrase which explain the strength and weakness of Thomas' great gift. "Style," observes Arnold, "is the most striking quality" of Welsh verse. "Celtic poetry," he continues, "seems to make up to itself for being unable to master the world and to give an adequate interpretation of it, by throwing all its force into style,

[22] The occasion of Thomas' statement was a review which Mr. Spender had written of the poet's *Collected Poems* in the *Spectator*. Thomas' appreciation of this notice was expressed in his letter. "You were," he wrote, "the very first person ever to write to me about a poem of mine; and this is now the clearest, most considered and sympathetic, and, in my opinion, truest review that I have ever seen of my writing. I mean, that your statement and understanding of my aim and method seems to me altogether true. . . ."

by bending language at any rate to its will, and expressing the ideas it has with unsurpassable intensity, elevation, and effect. It has all through it a sort of intoxication of style—a *Pindarism*, to use a word formed from the name of the poet, on whom, above all other poets, the power of style seems to have exercised an inspiring and intoxicating effect." How well this helps us to define the specific attraction of Thomas' verse; even as the following sentence suggests a certain lack of organising power, of self-administrative talent, both in the man and the poet. "The Celt," writes Arnold, "has not at all, in spite of his quick perception, the Latin talent for dealing with the fact, dexterously managing it and making himself master of it. . . . He is a quick genius, checkmated for want of strenuousness or else patience."

V

An acquaintance of the poet,[23] invited to a party at the house of Vernon Watkins where some Swansea intellectuals were present, remarked how amazed he was to find that Thomas was almost a legendary figure in his lifetime and among his friends. "For instance," he writes, "if they said of anyone—'He comes in the *Portrait of the Artist as a Young Dog*,' that was like tracing one of the characters in *Nightmare Abbey*."

In this biographical chapter, it is the combination of the man and the myth that I have been striving to express. My aim has been that of the 'spirit portrait' rather than that of the photographic likeness;[24] and I

[23] Mr. Charles David Ley.
[24] For the fullest detailed story, to date, of the poet's life, the reader is referred to Suzanne Rousillat's article *His Work and Background* in *Adam* no. 238 (1953).

should like to close with four impressions that are clearly personal to the authors who gave them.

Mr. Dennis Roberts remembers Thomas as one of the members of Victor Neuberg's *Sunday Referee* 'Poet's Corner' Group. The encouragement which Victor Neuberg and Mr. Mark Goulden (now a director of the publishers W. H. Allen, and in those days Editor of the *Sunday Referee*) offered to the young poet, whom they virtually 'discovered', has been described by Miss Runia Sheila Macleod;[25] and it is interesting to compare her portrait of the poet with that of Mr. Roberts.

"I remember him," writes the latter, "as a rather effeminate, sulky-looking youth who kept himself aloof from the rest of us. . . . On fine evenings we used to congregate in a neglected garden at the back of [Neuberg's] house and there read each other's poems aloud. I can see Dylan now, hands in pocket, perched up on some rockery . . . listening to our effusions with ill-concealed boredom." "A handsome cherubic youth, crowned with an aura of thunderous power and doom," is how Miss Macleod recalls him.

Again, when the poet gave a talk to the Oxford University Celtic Society in 1948, Mr. Keith Brace formed the following image of him: "He looked like a transcendental tinplate worker with his battered pork-pie hat and heavy belted overcoat, and dishevelled cigarette stub held most delicately in his fingers, spattering ash over his notes." Yet again, in a quite different key, is Dr. Edith Sitwell's[26] recollection of the poet: "He was not tall, but was extremely broad, and gave an impression of extraordinary strength, sturdiness, and superabundant life. (His reddish-amber curls, strong as the curls on the brow of a young bull, his proud, but not despising, bearing,

[25] *The Dylan I Knew* (*Adam* no. 238, 1953).
[26] *Dylan Thomas* (*The Atlantic* Feb. 1954).

emphasised this.) Mr. Augustus John's portrait of him is beautiful, but gives him a cherubic aspect, which, though pleasing, does not convey, to the present writer at least, Dylan's look of archangelic power."

With these different testimonies before one, it is easy to ask 'Who was the real Thomas?' The question is, indeed, a hard one; but I think the nearest answer has been given by A. G. Prys-Jones, in a tribute paid to the poet at the Memorial Recital organised by the Cardiff Branch of the Poetry Association.[27]

"Like most of us," he writes, "though more boldly and defiantly, he strode on two levels—he could be 'the brassy orator', the terrible boy with 'the lovely gift of the gab': he could be unreliable, unpredictable, awkward and irresponsible. In quick succession he could reveal the imp, the cherub, the poseur, the angel, the literary showman, the dedicated craftsman, all of whom lived within him in a state of perpetual civil war.

On his unconventional level he was the complete bohemian, scorning the accustomed virtues of respectability: and carrying his insignia of defiance unashamedly and sometimes provocatively—his seaman's jersey—his old tweed coat—his flannels—his cigarette and his pint. One can imagine him in the earlier Elizabethan age roaring and roystering with Thomas Prys and William Middleton, those full-blooded buccaneering Welsh poets, in the taverns of London and Llanrwst."

But he was always—in the end—lovable: and deep at heart he was humble and contrite, and immensely grateful for even small kindnesses. He was generous and forgiving, quite unworldly in the material sense, and like Blake vividly aware of the sacramental unity of the earth and all that dwelt therein. He hated, if he ever hated at all, only those who were cruel or unkind,

[27] Published in *Dock Leaves* (Pembroke) Spring, 1954.

stupid, or insincere. Despite all his waywardness, somehow or other, one got the impression that, rather mysteriously perhaps and by some special dispensation, he was always within a state of grace: and was allowed a much more liberal overdraft on the bank of God's patience and mercy than is given to most of us. Beneath his saloon panache and the brittle half-truths, the extravagant *obiter dicta* which he threw off like brilliant sparks in bar-rooms and lecture-halls, there lay just beneath the surface—the clear, still waters of a child-like innocence."

PART TWO

The Poems

18 Poems

I

WITH THE APPEARANCE of his volume *18 Poems*
in 1934 the first outlines of Thomas' imaginary world
were given. The area enclosed by those outlines constitutes the base of all his poetry. Time has extended
the boundaries somewhat; but the first premises and
intuitions which we encounter in this early book
serve as a guide to his later work. It is therefore
necessary to deal with these poems in some detail.

But, first, it may prove helpful to distinguish between
the poetry of Thomas and that of poets with cognate
interests. As we meet it in *18 Poems*, Thomas' poetry is
one of sexuality; but it is a sexual poetry very different
from that of many erotic poets. There is little in it, for
example, of Catullus' poetry of "odi et amo"—of the
pain and jealousy and anguish of desire. Such pieces
from the *Carmenina* of the Latin poet as LXX—

> but let what a woman says to her lover
> Be written in running water and told to the wind.[1]

or LVIII—

[1] & [2] Translated by Arthur Symons.

31

Caelius, Lesbia mine, that Lesbia, that
Lesbia whom Catullus for love did rate
Higher than all himself and than all things, stands
Now at the cross-roads and the alleys, to wait
For the lords of Rome, with public lips and hands.[2]

are quite alien to Thomas' poetry.

Foreign, also, to Thomas is D. G. Rossetti's poetry
of erotic vision, in which the physical and the spiritual
are so consumately combined and juxtaposed. Sonnets
from the sequence *The House of Life*, such as *Nuptial
Sleep, The Kiss*, or *Supreme Surrender* offer us the type of
this passionate romanticism. I quote the latter:

To all the spirits of love that wander by
    Along the love-sown fallowfield of sleep
    My lady lies apparent; and the deep
Calls to the deep; and no man sees but I.
The bliss so long afar, at length so nigh,
    Rests there attained. Methinks proud Love must weep
    When Fate's control doth from his harvest reap
The sacred hour for which the years did sigh.

First touched, the hand now warm around my neck
    Taught memory long to mock desire: and lo!
    Across my breast the abandoned hair doth flow,
Where one shorn tress long stirred the longing ache:
And next the heart that trembled for its sake
    Lies the queen-heart in sovereign overthrow.

Neither does Thomas' poetry treat of that ideal
imaginary lust which provided Swinburne with so
many themes:

I would find grevious ways to have thee slain,
Intense device, and superflux of pain;
Vex thee with amorous agonies, and shake
Life at thy lips, and leave it there to ache;
Strain out thy soul with pangs too soft to kill,
Intolerable interludes, and infinite ill;
Relapse and reluctation of the breath
                                    (*Anactoria*)

Nor yet have his poems affinity with the sensuous romantic passion of Keats (as in the *Eve of St. Agnes* or the sonnets to Fanny Brawne), or with Shelley's sensuous transcendental passion (as in *Epipsychidion*).

I have chosen to cite these poets because, as authors of sexual poetry, their work refers back to a body of verse which each, respectively, has behind him. The kind of interest they evince in the relationship of the sexes, and their elaborations on this interest, form part of a separate given stream of thought and expression on the subject. In that sense, they are traditionally-minded.

When we come to Thomas' poems, the presence of a body of like-minded poetry to serve as referendum cannot be located. As I shall try to establish, there are elements of traditional thought discoverable in his poetry which are not readily perceived as bearing upon matters of sex. As a sexual poet, Thomas first strikes us by his apparent complete originality; and the difficulty we encounter in first reading him springs from a powerful inventiveness of speech corresponding to his unique and singular apprehension of life.

Perhaps we can begin our approach to Thomas by saying that his poems reveal a less adulterated interest in sex than that of most erotic poets. His subject is pure sexuality, rather than sex as understood in its relation to love or lust. One of the clearest proofs of this, is the part that conception and gestation occupy in his poetry. For the majority of erotic poets, the concern with the processes of sex ends with the act of physical congress.

> Whoever loves, if he do not propose
> The right true end of love, he's one that goes
> To sea for nothing but to make him sick.[3]

writes Donne, who takes the customary view of the

[3] An entirely masculine view of the matter, it may be remarked.

matter. But between "the right true end of love" and the chain of physical consequences resulting from an act of union there is an important difference.[4]

Thomas' interest is with this latter, more natural, and 'unabridged' process. With him, the sexual image in a poem always has the reproductive end in view. Thus, in many of the *18 Poems*, the seed of man addresses us in its role of child-to-be. This *persona* of the poet does not speak with the brief voice of desire, of the male impulse hastily seeking its own transitory gratification, but expresses itself in terms of the future embryo, of a fresh additional particle of life.

But though the poet's concern is with the unabbreviated workings of sex, his poetry does not represent the erotic life more fully than others. The chief cause of this, in *18 Poems*, is that Thomas depersonalises the acts and circumstances of sex. The lovers in *18 Poems* are not two human personalities, but rather two polarised genitary tracts—two articulate procreative and reproductive regions. In other words, in his first book of poems, Thomas severs sexuality from most of the issues of individual love. The severance appears of a drastic order, and bears some resemblance to what D. H. Lawrence effected in certain of his novels.[5] But

[4] The reason why the majority of erotic poets have located "the right true end of love" in physical intercourse between the partners, rather than in children—the fruit of such acts—is not, perhaps, hard to seek. So many of them were unmarried men, and the loves they wrote of so often outside marriage, that the thought of offspring could only be a burden, as well as a grave deterrent to the lady whose favours they were courting.

This tendency was also strengthened by the conditions in which the concept of romantic passion-love took its rise in Europe. Both in ancient Rome and in Provence, marriage was generally equated with the advancement of prosperity than with the fulfilment of mutual desire. The troubadours, who did so much to formulate the idea of romantic passion, often addressed their love-songs to the wife of another (who was frequently their feudal superior), sometimes without much hope of response.

To discover the poetic ethos in which "the right true end of love" and the physical consequences of sex are not set apart but taken together, we have to return to the Old Testament; as, for instance, in the stories of Abraham and Sara, and Jacob and Leah.

[5] *The Plumed Serpent* particularly; and in part *The Lost Girl* and *Lady Chatterley's Lover*.

whereas, whether for better or worse, Lawrence's later treatment of sex constitutes a revision of love, Thomas' account of it in *18 Poems* was the product of a first view. The outcome of a young man of twenty, the book bears all the marks of an unhappy sexual precocity; all the symptoms of that physical troubling of the mind which belong to the years of adolescence.

It is important, then, not to take the *18 Poems* as offering a critique of love. The natural encounter of two pubic parts and the tale of the aftermath of their meeting, however vividly described, does not comprise a figure of human affection. But just this obsessed youthful short-sightedness which—through its concentration on salient physical features—makes its vision of love so one-sided, just this serves to inaugurate the metaphysical exploration of sex which Thomas undertook.

One of the paradoxes of the poet consists in this latter achievement. Superficially, his poems present no more than an intense narrow picture of sex, in which there is no room for a description of human love. But although the *18 Poems* are exclusively physical in comment, this physical element is generalised to an unprecedented extent. If, then, Thomas' poetry is one of sexuality, this sexuality must not be regarded in that special isolated fashion in which most sexologists understand their subject. What Thomas' poetry does is to locate the human sexual process against a cosmic background which repeats the sexual pattern. Another way of saying this is, that Thomas has a vision of the world as body. To him, the universe is sexual, as when he writes:

> And yellow was the multiplying sand
> Each golden grain spat life into its fellow

or

> All all and all the dry world's lever,
> Stage of the ice, the solid ocean,
> All from the oil the pound of lava

or

> All all and the dry worlds couple

or

> Life rose and spouted from the rolling seas,
> Burst in the roots, pumped from the earth and rock
> The secret oils that drive the grass.

George Santayana, in his book *Winds of Doctrine*, remarks how "in the *Prometheus* Shelley has allowed his fancy, half in symbol, half in glorious physical hyperbole, to carry the warm contagion of love into the very bowels of the earth, and even the moon, by reflection, to catch the light of love, and be alive again." If, in this passage, we replace the word 'love' with the word 'sex', we have a good account of the fashion in which Thomas conceives the universe.

I am not urging that the poet would have held with such a formulation in the absolute sense, or that he would have maintained it as a doctrine intellectually. But for our own purpose, and for his as a poet, we can say that such a scheme of the world has the force of poetic truth.

In order to refer to this mode of sexually perceiving the cosmos, I intend—for short-hand reasons—to resort to an hypothesis, the supposition of pantheism. Now pantheism, in Bertrand Russell's definition, "holds that God and the world are not distinct, and that everything in the world is part of God."[6] This being so, the world and all things in it are separately yet reciprocally alive; or—in the words of Coleridge—

[6] *History of Western Philosophy.*

there is "for every object . . . a sort of life, and passions and motions attending it."[7]

From this, there follows the corollary that in all our dealings with matter, we are actually dealing with God. But if in dealing with one sort of matter, we are dealing with God just as much as if we had to do with matter of a different sort, then all matter, religiously speaking, must be interchangeable.

Whatever may be the practical consequences of believing in such a doctrine, the poetic consequence is simple. The image of matter of one kind can easily stand for matter of another. So, in the poem *Into her Lying Down Head* (from the volume *Deaths and Entrances*) the lovers in section one are replaced in section three by

> Two sand grains together in bed
> Head to heaven-circling head

who repeat the actions of the lovers and are, accordingly, identified with them.

When, therefore, the poet deals with matter of one kind or another, he is dealing with, partaking of, God; and when he substitutes for the image of this matter the image of matter of a different type, he is creating a sacrament, and establishing a sacramental view of the world. In the *Book of Common Prayer*, a sacrament is defined as "an outward and visible sign of an inward and spiritual grace"; and in a ready way this applies to the poetry of Thomas. A fuller definition, however, is to be found in the writings of the seventeenth-century Anglican Divine, Edward Reynolds. "The nature of a sacrament," he writes, "is to be the representative of a substance, the sign of a covenant, the seal of a purchase, the figure of a body, the witness of our faith, the earnest of our hope, the presence of things distant, the sign of things absent, the taste of

[7] *Philosophical Lectures 1818–1819*, ed. Kathleen Coburn.

things inconceivable, and the knowledge of things that are past knowledge." All this remarkably describes the manner of thought and the use of images in Thomas' poetry; as when in *This bread I break* (from *25 Poems*), he speaks of the bread "which was once the oat", and which—after sustaining him—is partaken of in turn by his sweetheart in their act of love together. I think this sacramental hypothesis will help us in our reading of the poet.

In his book on Thomas, Henry Treece has spoken of the "foetal unity" of *18 Poems*. This is an original and taking phrase; but not quite accurate statistically. *Especially when the October wind* deals with the making of a poem; *My hero bares his nerves* is about onanism; *In the beginning* concerns the creation of the universe; and the subject of *Our eunuch dreams* is the escapism and self-deception of many modes and thoughts of love.

Yet, in a fashion, Henry Treece is right; for what the majority of these poems do is to explore their subject's origin. *If I were tickled by the rub of love*—a search by the poet for his basic subject-matter—reveals the source of poetic experience in the quite Augustan line, "Man be my metaphor". *The force that through the green fuse drives the flower* is a similar quest; this time, for the common physical law that controls the natural and human worlds. So possibly it would be more precise to say that the principal subject of *18 Poems* is genesis: a return to the beginning of things.[8]

On the other hand, Treece's phrase very effectively focuses our mind on what is the upper-most recurrent image in these poems: namely, the image of the womb. In this at-first fantastic world, children address us from the bellies of their mothers, from their father's seed

---

[8] Those who find in such an attitude and method nothing but primitivism might well consider Aristotle's observation that "we shall not obtain the best insight into things until we actually see them growing from the beginning."

in the course of emission, or from the sleeping minds
of their sires before a dream has communicated a
generative impulse to the nerves:

> I fellowed sleep who kissed me in the brain,
> Let fall the tear of time; the sleeper's eye,
> Shifting to light, turned on me like a moon.

A fantastic world, no doubt; but if we accept the
anthropomorphic manner of thought that leads the
animals in La Fontaine's *Fables* to behave and dis-
course like men, or the Sensitive Plant in Shelley's
poem to pine for love like a genteel Platonist, then
surely Thomas is within his rights in presenting us with
a universe where the anthropomorphic imagination
concerns itself with the origins of man: the ovum, the
embryo, the homunculus, the seed.

II

"Many a time," wrote Baudelaire, in a letter to a
friend, "I have found myself wishing that the poet
. . . could enjoy the pleasure of a museum of love
where everything would have a place from the tenderness of Saint Teresa . . . to the serious debauches
of the age of boredom."

Thomas' work certainly does not present us with
anything so aloofly aesthetic, so purely objective, as
"a museum of love". His poems are more like incidents
in a maternity-clinic or the operating-theatre of a
lying-in hospital, told from the view-point of the
patient.

But by now I have talked quite enough of the
general currents and tendencies to be found in Thomas'
work. And these tendencies or currents, being the
fruits of intuition rather than of abstract intellectual
thought, any philosophical précis of them must not

be taken for the poetry itself. They help to give us our bearings, but they are not to be mistaken for the landscape. We can only get our 'feel' of this by entering the country of the poet's text. The safest way of proceeding, therefore, is to deal with a number of his poems more minutely.

Poem one[9] ("I see the boys of summer") is a *resumé* of the greater part of Thomas' sexual poetry. Many themes or *motifs* appear in it: onanism, homosexuality, the pre-natal life, chiefly. But what holds the poem together is an atmospheric unity, produced by the persisting mood of physical excitement, combined with a dark sense of predestination. The poem is written in three sections, and section three opens with almost the identical sentence ("I see you boys of summer in your ruin") with which the poem, in section one, opens ("I see the boys of summer in their ruin").[10]

The poem cannot be said to progress in the sense of arriving at any conclusion which was not implicit in its setting-out. In all three sections the note of sterility, of self-destruction, and perversity, is struck. In section one we hear of the "gold tithings laid barren"; in section two we read of "the dark deniers" and of "the man of straw"; and in section three, of "the sons of flint and pitch" and that "Man in his maggot's barren".

The two first stanzas of section one seem to refer to onanism, or at least to a form of unnatural, and therefore sterile, love-making.

---

[9] In the original edition of *18 Poems* the poems were numbered. In *Collected Poems* they have as titles generally the first line, or part of the first line, of the poem. Hereafter, they will be referred to by me as they appear in this latter address.

[10] It is possible that the significance of the change from "the boys . . ." to "you boys . . ." marks a progress in greater intimacy, which the examination of the theme through two stanzas has effected. "You" may also mark a closer identification of the poet with his subject, as compared with the more general, non-committal article, "the".

> I see the boys of summer in their ruin
> Lay the gold tithings barren,
> Setting no store by harvest, freeze the soils;
> There in their heat the winter floods
> Of frozen loves they fetch their girls,
> And drown the cargoed apples in their tides.

In primitive societies the expenditure of sexual energy was often regulated by tribal laws. In modern times the practical taboos of early sexual hygiene have largely been lost; but in its place we have inherited a partly unlocated sense of guilt, such as can be felt in the above stanzas. It is to acts of auto-erethism that this feeling of guilt is predominantly attached, but the normal intercourse of the sexes can also produce it. My point is, that Thomas, in his thought, is very much a primitive type; and it would therefore be wrong to interpret the expression of guilt in his poems as necessarily referring to auto-erotic or homosexual practices, solely.

But in stanza three of this section the idea of gestation and pregnancy appear:

> I see the summer children in their mothers
> Split up the brawned womb's weathers,

The pre-natal life of the child in the womb, which, according to a certain school of psychology determines so great a part of our nervous make-up, is one of Thomas' poetic preoccupations. In an age of hedonism such as ours, the significance of gestation and birth, as the true fulfilment of the sex-life of woman, has tended to be under-rated by many theorists. Very few poets have taken this subject, or even touched on it incidentally. Anne Ridler's volume of poems *Nine Bright Shiners* (1943) (a reference to the months of pregnancy) is a notable exception; but it is to be doubted whether this volume would have appeared if Thomas had not pioneered in the field of 'body' poetry nine years earlier. What Thomas offers us, here, are the over-sights of the rationalistic scientific mind corrected by the powers of intuition. "Birth, copulation, and death" are present in a cyclic manner in his poems, and shown as dependant upon each other. Hence onanism (which in terms of productive sexual energy represents a kind of death) appears side by side in a poem where birth is also a subject.

Neither does this intrusion of the idea of fruitfulness, in a poem which has hitherto canvassed its images of sterility, in any way serve to break the circle; for in the fourth stanza of the first section "the summer children in their mothers" have become "these boys" from whom "men of nothing" will grow. The cyclic doom of the physical life, from birth to death, is stressed once more; and stressed as Thomas often stresses it by the onastic image of self-destruction:

> I see that from these boys shall men of nothing
> Stature by seedy shifting,
> Or lame the air with leaping from its heats;

The last three lines of this stanza, I take it, speak of the barren expenditure of energy ("expense of spirit in a waste of shame", as Shakespeare expressed it in a different context). The "pulse of summer" is present, but it throbs only "in the ice", because the world of the onanist is cold, void, and unreceptive. The ice stands for the condition of the onanist's unpartnered state.

Section two seems the most mixed and fluctuating of all three sections in terms of its thought. There are images of perversity ("Here break a kiss in no love's quarry"); images of negativity—possibly onanistic ("We are the dark deniers", "Here love's damp muscle dries and dies"); an image which may perhaps stand for the onanist's compulsion-neurosis ("punctual as death" suggests this reading, as do other lines in this section).

There is also in this section the urge towards, and hope for, normal sexual congress:

> let us summon
> Death from a summer woman,
> A muscling life from lovers in their cramp.

The third stanza, though, has an 'all-male cast', which makes it appear as if the poem has reverted to the idea of onanism and homosexuality.

The last stanza has some sacrificial meaning (the image of the "merry squires" standing in place of the Christ figure). It is likely enough that the "merry squires" symbolise the male organ, since the poet often refers to it in a jocular manner[11] ("the knobbly ape", "cherry-capped dangler"). But whether the orgasmic process be thought of in terms of onanism or of normal intercourse, it represents for the male a sort of crucifixion, a yielding-up of his spirit; hence the idea of nailing to a tree.

The last line of the stanza offers again the potentiality for normal sexuality, which the import of the concluding section destroys:

> I see you boys of summer in your ruin.
> Man in his maggot's barren.
> And boys are full and foreign in the pouch.
> I am the man your father was.
> We are the sons of flint and pitch.
> O see the poles are kissing as they cross.

In these last six lines, the theme of sterility (through homosexuality and onanistic practice) is emphatically stated:

> Man in his maggot's barren.
> And boys are full and foreign in the pouch.

[11] His other mood of reference is the reverse. With a Gothic morbidity, he speaks of it as a "worm", "maggot", and "quick".

The vicious circle established by the past is shown as controlling the present: "I am the man your father was"; and the heredity of untender physical love and physical corruption is suggested in the phrase, "We are the sons of flint and pitch." Finally, there comes the undeniable damnatory image of homosexual action,

> O see the poles are kissing as they cross

which winds up the poem.

The next piece in Thomas' first volume, *Where once the twilight locks no longer*, shares with the poem just quoted a like fluctuation of vantage-points.

The poem is written in the first person, but the 'I' who speaks seems at one moment to be the child in the womb; at another, its mother; and, at a third, the father. Perhaps the most helpful way of thinking of the speaker is to imagine him as a figure similar to T. S. Eliot's Tiresias, "old man with wrinkled female breast."[12] In Thomas' poem, however, he is young; but, like Eliot's Tiresias, he has "foresuffered all": not only the woman's experience of conception, pregnancy, and child-birth; nor the man's experience of the sexual act; but that of the pre-conscious child in the womb. Thomas' fluctuating and amorphous figure (the child behind the voice which speaks, in this poem, in the third person) is more complex than the hermaphrodite: it is the human trinity (father, mother, and child, in one).

The first stanza seems to tell of the child's experience. "The twilight locks" that "no lònger/Locked in the long worm of my finger" refers to the child's delivery; the "locks" being, I assume, either the pelvis or the mouth of the womb.

---

[12] In the poem *Before I knocked* the unconceived child also features as a sort of Tiresias-figure. This being is described as "brother to Mnetha's daughter And sister to the fathering worm." This appears to me a poetic way of stating that the seed of the male is neither male nor female. The poet affirmatively makes it both.

The transitions of reference in stanza two are so rapid, merging so strangely into each other, that it is difficult to follow the sequence. "The galactic sea", in the first line, is the milk-filled breast of the mother; and when the poet speaks of it as being sucked, it indicates a period after the child's birth. But there is an ambiguity in the third and fourth line; for in the first instance "globe" seems to stand for the world, while the "globe . . . of hair and bone" in the second case probably refers to the father's organ ("My father's globe", the poet writes in another poem). The "flask of matter" is the child as embryo, but it is strange to read of this foetus strung to "his rib" (instead of to the mother's). I think we can explain this latter as being part of the poet's *anticipative* vision: the child can be thought of as being strung to the father's rib, since from his body comes the seed which fertilises the child-to-be.

The words of stanza three seem to be placed in the mouth of the woman, as there is mention of "his heart", "his father's magics" (and not 'my father's', which would be the foetus' form of address).

The fourth stanza is both vague and violent.

> Some dead undid their bushy jaws,
> And bags of blood let out their flies

suggests the act of birth.

The last three stanzas effect a shift of perspective that makes it even harder to focus on a meaning. In the first of these it is probably quite impossible to construct a single consistent meaning.

"The dry Sargasso of the tomb" that gives up its dead may be the unfertilised ova of the womb that are discharged by menstruation ("a working sea"), or it may be the cells made quick by the "working sea" of invading sperm ("fishes' food", with its olefactory suggestion, may be a reference to semen). "Periscope", in the sixth line, rather indicates the upward movement of the male organ. It is strange to find this verb attached to the unsubstantial subject "shades", but the noun may be meant to convey the idea of the spirits of children-to-be contained in the ascending globule of seed.

Whether "my ambassador" in the next stanza is the child travelling downward to the "light" of birth, or the male member travelling upwards (but why to "light"?), it is hard to say.

The second reading is more in keeping with the stanza as a whole. We are told that the "ambassador" fell asleep", "And conjured up a carcase shape", which may be rendered into prose as 'rested after the effort of sex by which a child was conceived'. "To rob me of my fluids in his heart" may have been spoken by the man or the woman, since both have contributed to the child's creation.

The last stanza appears to be addressed to the child, exhorting him to enter the world. "The poppied pick-thank" who lies at rest is presumably the same object as the "ambassador" who "fell asleep" in the last stanza, namely, the tired male member ("poppied" suggesting both its colour and its sleepy sated condition, and "pickthank" one who effects an entry and is thanked for so doing).

The last three lines of this stanza speak of the aftermath to the night of procreation. All but "the briskest riders" (the most vigorous males) are exhausted. The "world" hanging on the trees may be an image of futurity, the fruit of yet-unplucked experience, or of the fertilised or unfertilised ova remaining in the womb.

If, to return to the words of Goethe, we say that *When once the twilight locks no longer* is "as a whole . . . intelligible, but in some particulars a little unintelligible", we cannot admit to finding this central column of meaning in all Thomas' poems. Sometimes the absence of this central meaning is found in a poem which appears to mean too much; for to seem to mean all things is to mean nothing. Such is the case with *A process in the weather of the heart*—a poem about a law or "process" that controls all things in the cosmos. But, unlike *The force that through the green fuse drives the flower* (a poem dealing with the same thought), there are no fixed images to serve as referenda or vantage-points; or, rather, there are too many of them, and they have no stability of meaning. "A process in the weather of the heart", "A process in the eye", "A darkness in the weather of the eye", "A weather in the flesh and bone", and "A process in the weather of the world" are all poetically equated; and as none of them are defined, the sum of this equation is that $o = o$.

A second reason for a central absence of meaning, in some of Thomas' poems, is the balanced ambiguity they sometimes reveal. Thus, in *Where once the waters of your face*, it is difficult to know whether the subject of the poem is a woman or a boat. The 'double-focus' of the opening is maintained by two strands of imagery; one drawn from maritime ("mermen", "salt", "knots", "tides") and the other from domestic ("lovebeds", "children") experience.

Of the pieces in *18 Poems* dealing with pre-natal existence, *Before I knocked* is both the clearest and most lyrical. The poem speaks of the life of the child prior even to its conception (just as another poem *I fellowed sleep* traces its origin to an impulse in the father's dreaming brain).

The poet imagines the spirit of the child "shapeless as the water"—a kind of impalpable brooding presence which the act of sex has not yet brought into focus.

... Ungotten I knew night and day.

There is also a vivid description of 'the child', from

the point of view of its own being during the moment
of coitus:

> I who was deaf to spring and summer,
> Who knew not sun nor moon by name,
> Felt thud beneath my flesh's armour,
> As yet was in a molten form,
> The leaden stars, the rainy hammer
> Swung by my father from his dome.

The image of the unconceived child's flesh as
"molten" (like the warm amorphous seminal fluid)
and of the phallus as "the rainy hammer", with "the
leaden stars" (where the adjective phonetically suggests
the state of being laden) as the drops of ejaculated seed
are examples of high poetic inventiveness. Processes of
energy and energy's transmission take on the appearance of things created. Forces are as substantially
expressed as objects belonging to the world of 'solids'.

One of the poem's important aspects is its statement
of the community of all things. This unity of the human
spirit and all created matter is shown as existing before
birth.

The cyclic unity of birth and death is also stated in
the poem. Even before the child was born:

> My heart knew love, my belly hunger;
> I smelt the maggot in my stool.

The last stanza goes some way towards expressing a
sacramental view of man and God (according to
Christian thought):

> You who bow down at cross and altar,
> Remember me and pity Him
> Who took my flesh and bone for armour
> And doublecrossed my mother's womb.

Christ, as orthodox doctrine tells us, took on the
likeness of man, and may be said to have "double-

crossed" his "mother's womb" in two senses: one, literally in the sense of cheating her by being himself conceived of the Holy Ghost (a being without physical attributes); and, two, in the sense of having twice crossed it—first, in the form of the Holy Spirit by whom she was made pregnant; and, secondly, in the form of the Son of God whom she bore (for the Trinity are "Three in One, and One in Three".).

We notice, also, in this stanza that the Christian Communion-idea of remembering Christ is reversed by the poet: man is to be remembered and Christ to be pitied. The thought of this conscious reversal stems perhaps from a strong attraction in the poet to the person of an unrisen Christ (an attitude quite common to-day, and one which much religious art manifests).

In its language the poem has unusual clarity; and the third stanza contains two of the loveliest simple epithets in recent English poetry ("The darted hail, the childish snow"). The wind as a "sister suitor" has the graceful and alliterative touch of some of Swinburne's best phrases. The "hellborn dew" is, for me, the only verbal mistake in the poem, suggesting as it does a variation on the banal image of hell-brew from a witch's cauldron. Had the idea of Original Sin been otherwise developed in the poem, this image might better have fallen into place.

My world is pyramid is another 'womb' poem. Section one describes the conception of a child through the joint energies of the man and woman. The child is destined to be a cripple, since the seed of the father was a "Corrosive spring out of the iceberg's crop". The last two stanzas of this section seem a muddle of motives and images.

Both in the first and second sections of the poem, in the term "pyramidal" I think there is a reference to the archtypal human trinity of father, mother, and child.

From love's first fever to her plague covers a larger area of human experience. It tells the story of love's evolution, from the conception of the child to the child's eventual awareness of sex. It is also an account of the way in which the unitive vision of childhood yields to the adult's multiple vision. When the child's world "was christened in a stream of milk",

> earth and sky were as one airy hill,
> The sun and moon were one white light.

But this is superseded by "the divorcing sky" of adolescent consciousness, whose "two-framed globe [of night and day] spun into a score".

The poem contains a powerful image of physical decay:

> The root of tongues end in a spentout cancer

—growth towards life or growth towards death are often equated in Thomas's poetry: the law of the conservation of matter is ironically illustrated in his work.

I dreamed my genesis reverses the process of most of these 'womb' poems, where the child or the seed dreams of its life to come. Here, however, the poet looks back, dreaming his act of birth over again. The dream continues, and as it develops he pre-experiences his death in war. But from this death once more he rises, undergoing a second birth.

The piece looks forward to Thomas' great hymnal lyric, in *25 Poems*, *And death shall have no dominion*; but has neither its spiritual nor literary strength.

Closely connected in Thomas' mind with the inception of human life was the theme of the evolution of the world. Several poems deal with this. The first three stanzas of *In the beginning* offer a religiously sexual account of creation. "In the beginning was the

three-pointed star", besides offering an astrological
symbol, containing a reference to the mystic number—three—points to the human trinity (of father,
mother, and child) and the triune God who created the
world.

In stanza four of the poem we get the poet's own
interpretation of the first verse of the Gospel of St.
John ("In the beginning was the Word, and the Word
was with God, and the Word was God").

Thomas offers us the Gospel of St. John with God
omitted and the part of the Baptist played by the poet.
According to him, it is the word that has created meaning in the universe. It is rather like Arnold's Bible
without God.

This mythopœic process is best seen in his poem
Especially when the October wind. It is poetry about the
making of a poem (a subject Yeats, too, was fond of),
and of how the creation of this microcosm reflects
back on the larger world without.

It is one of Thomas' finest pieces, and is describable
as an incantatory landscape composition. But it is not
a 'nature poem' in the accepted sense of the word, for
there are touches of 'domestic interior' scene-painting
("Behind a pot of ferns the wagging clock. . . ."), as
well as 'mindscapes' of the poet's own nature:

> My busy heart who shudders as she talks
> Shakes the syllabic blood and drains her words.

Another way of speaking of the poem—and one
where the relevance of my first statement about it
becomes apparent—would be to call it a *wordscape*;
for, in some sense, in this poem, to the poet words are
the reallest things. Thus, he talks of himself as "shut
. . . in a tower of words" and observes "The windy
shapes of women".

This latter example, I feel, carries a suggestion of the
sight of women chatting; but there still remains the

implication in which "windy shapes" is equatable with 'word-like shapes'. Now the point is, that women are not word-like in appearance—save to the poet, who sees everything potentially as words. A third example of this word-consciousness is his mention of "the vowelled beeches". It is true that the word which describes the tree is verbally well endowed with vowels, but the description fits the word and not the object which it stands for. As trees, not words, beeches are not "vowelled".

Just as many of Thomas' poems deal with the pro-creative forces of sex at work in the poet, so this poem (outwardly a landscape-piece) records the creative powers of poetry working on the poet in favourable circumstances.

The first six lines of the first stanza describe the conditions which have led the poet's "busy heart" to shed its "syllabic blood". These lines are remarkable for a distribution of vivid phrases. The October wind "punishes" the poet's hair. The autumn sun is "crabbing" (red like a crab), and under its light the poet walks "on fire" and casts "a shadow crab upon the land". This time the metaphor refers to the crab's shape and gait, not its colour: the shadow of a man crawls crab-wise on the earth.

The second stanza comes closer to identifying the landscape and its objects with the words the poet uses to describe them. Women walking on the horizon are seen as trees, not only on account of the visual similarity, but because both of them are reducible to "wordy shapes". "The star-gestured children in the park" vividly depicts the playing youngsters, their arms excitedly flung out, in the course of their games, giving them the momentary appearance of five-pointed stars.

The last four lines of this stanza shows how implicated the thought of this poem is:

> Some let me make you of the vowelled beeches,
> Some of the oaken voices, from the roots
> Of many a thorny shire tell you notes,
> Some let me make you of the water's speeches.

"Some" stands for 'words' or 'word-shapes'; so that, in effect, what the poet is saying, is: 'Let me make you words or word-shapes out of the beech-trees, the oaks, and the sound of running water.'

In the third stanza the scene shifts to the interior of a room where the poet is writing. The clock ("wagging" because of its pendulum, moving from side to side like a dog's tail) behind the "pot of ferns", with all its lower-middle-class associations, provides a good contrast to the more 'poetic' décor of the first two stanzas. The next four lines seem to contain partly redundant material:

> Behind a pot of ferns the wagging clock
> Tells me the hour's word, the neural meaning
> Flies on the shafted disk, declaims the morning
> And tells the windy weather in the cock.

The clock tells the time, to the eye and to the ear; and the significance or inner meaning of that time is what makes the cock crow. The poet, always on the look-out for the law behind the appearance of things, distinguishes between time as a phenomenon or measure (something read on the dials of clocks) and time as something with a cosmic meaning (a force which provides the morning, and constitutes cockerels so that they greet it). I cannot, however, admire the passage, which seems circumlocutory, with one word particularly out of place, "neural" (whose definition is "pertaining to nerves"). "The neural meaning" of time which is recorded on the clock's dial seems a vague or unmeaningful idea. Perhaps the poet is thinking of the second-hand (of a small clock) or the minute-hand (of a larger one) jerking forward like twitching nerves. Another meaning possible here (though hardly justified by the true definition of "neural") is that of an 'inner meaning' as opposed to the 'surface meaning' which the dial of the clock offers. The poet may have equated "neural" with 'inner' in his mind because nerves are beneath the surface of the skin. If this explanation is correct, Thomas' purport is that the 'inner meaning' of time is expressed by the 'surface meaning' in terms of the digits of hours and minutes. But in whatever way we choose to read it, the phrase can hardly be accounted a success.

Neither, on the whole, can the last stanza. As with many of Thomas' poems, there is no form of definite advance, only a form of repetition which is not even circular in its treatment of a theme. The incantatory intention of the poem (the suggestion of its being a kind of magical procedure) is borne out by the phrase "autumnal spells", of which "The spider-tongued, and the loud hills of Wales" are seen as the principal ingredients. The land, punished by the "October wind" "with fists of turnips" is a cogent image, stronger even than its counter-part in line two of the first stanza.

But from the fifth line of this last stanza the meaning becomes vague or tautological. "Some let me make you of the heartless words" writes the poet; but if, in this sentence (as I have suggested in an early parallel passage of the poem), "Some" stands for 'words' or 'word-shapes', the line is superflous. And if we substitute 'poem' for 'word-shapes' we are not offered anything very exciting—merely, poems made of "heartless words".

The next two lines speak of the gestation and delivery of the poem in typical physical terms. But the points of reference remain dim and solipsistic. If the "coming fury" refers to the poem raging in the poet as it waits to be 'born', and if "spelling in the scurry/Of chemic blood" represents the process of putting it down on paper, then the poet has said something like the following: 'The feeling that foretold me a poem was on its way is now exhausted, since the poem has been written'. This, naturally, is a bare-faced *précis*; and a *précis* is not the equal of a poem or of a poetic statement; but if it can show that a poetic statement is as self-obvious as this one seems to be, I doubt if we can care very much for the original.

It is feasible, though, that "the coming fury" of the poem was intended, by the poet, to be equated with "the coming fury" of the sea-gulls' cries down by the shore ("By the sea's side hear the dark-vowelled birds"), or with the noise of the sea in general. In other words, 'the feeling that foretold the cry of gulls is exhausted now in the composition of the poem'.

This alternative reading implicates the last line with the preceding three more satisfactorily but still leaves us with little more than an 'autospective' poetical musing. Like many of Thomas' poems, this fine piece has an inadequate end.

Especially when the October wind shows the poet at the task of composition: *If I were tickled by the rub of love* deals with his search for proper subject-matter, for a starting-off point of poetic thought which shall serve as a touch-stone to him.

The words "If I were tickled by . . ." are to be given two connotations: one, 'amused by' (which picks up "the midnight of a chuckle" in the sixth stanza of the poem), and, two, 'captivated by', 'caught up in', almost 'taken in by'.

The poet appears to begin by saying that if he were thoroughly involved in, thoroughly preoccupied with, love, onanism, or creation, the circumstances that bring these matters to an end would not fill him with fear; but, as it is,

> I sit and watch the worm beneath my nail
> Wearing the quick away.

He is always conscious of mutability, since no obsession can hold him from reflection. And this sense of the fleetingness of things is "the rub, the only rub that tickles". The thought of change alone can fasten all the poet's attention on itself. Compared with this issue "The knobbly ape that swings along his sex" (erotic activity), "Can never raise the midnight of a chuckle". Or, in the vernacular, 'love has got nothing on death'.

In the last stanza, the poet describes how this very real "rub" (the apprehension of change and death in all things) reflects back on all human behaviour, darkening it with a future shadow:

> And what's the rub. Death's feather on the nerve?
> Your mouth, my love, the thistle in the kiss?
> My Jack of Christ born thorny on the tree?
> The words of death are drier than his stiff,
> My wordy wounds are printed with your hair.
> I would be tickled by the rub that is:
> Man be my metaphor.

'I would occupy myself with the final issue that counts', the poet says in the one-but-last line; and, then, rather abruptly, 'Let me take man as my image of mutability'.

We must admire the cogency and economy of this close. "Man be my metaphor" is certainly more poetic than Pope's more rationalistic statement, "The proper study of mankind is man".

There is an image of onanism in this last poem: ..

> If I were tickled by the urchin hungers
> Rehearsing heat upon a raw-edged nerve.

and in *My hero bares his nerves* it becomes the entire subject. The poem describes an act of masturbation;

and "My hero" refers, with that unhappy Rabelaisian jocularity which Thomas sometimes employs, to the male member.

> Stripping my loin of promise,
> He promises a secret heat.
>
> .   .   .   .
>
> And tells the page the empty ill.

speaks of the vacant experience of the onanist. The final line

> He pulls the chain, the cistern moves.

suggests both the termination of the physical act and the literal gesture performed after it.

There is, in this last line, a sense of bathos, which does not fit the heroic or semi-heroic style of the poem ("Unpacks the head that, like a sleepy ghost/Leans on my mortal ruler,/The proud spine spurning turn and twist"), but, none the less, most aptly describes the void and slightly nauseous aftermath of the act; which appears, at its termination, not as an expression of human integration (as is the act of love) but as a function similar to defecation.

This death-side or 'death-life' of love exerts a strong fascination on the poet, especially in his first two books. The first four sections of *Our eunuch dreams* present us with different aspects of the illusion of love. 'Illusion' perhaps is not so much the word as 'mirage'; for the partners in these acts of love, which the poem describes to us, are all insubstantial unreal forms. They are all cheating erotic phantoms.

In section one, the phantom appears in the guise of a succubus—the female form which visits the dream of men. The two key-words in this section are "eunuch' and "seedless": "eunuch" because of the impossibility of intercourse where the partner is only a dream; and "seedless" because, though there may be seed, it can never spring to embryonic life.

Corresponding to these masculine key-words are the feminine terms "brides "and "widows". And these words are in apposition to each other, because the "dark brides" of an empty erotic dream are substantially unreal beings, and therefore incapable of receiving love. Hence they are "the widows of the night".

The first section, and indeed the two following, constitute a criticism, from the stand-point of actual love, of the modes which phantasmal and imagined love take. "Light and love", in the second line of the first stanza, are identical. Together, they represent reality—love which truly consummates and unifies, and light which honestly shows things as they are.

In section two, phantasmal love is presented in terms of the film-star lovers: those spectres of the erotic which haunt and yield their meagre satisfactions to many:

> We watch the show of shadows kiss or kill,
> Flavoured of celluloid give love the lie.

The emphasis again is one on the emptiness of these "one-dimensioned" antics.

The third section suggests that the sense of unreality has spread. 'Which is the real world?' asks the poet, 'That which we possess in dreams, or that which our waking hours offer?'

The last four lines of the poem offer yet another of love's unrealities. This time, "the bride" is a photograph, and in the first two lines of the stanza there is an indication of fetishism.

The fourth and concluding section summarises the unreal; and arrives at the thought that "This is the world" which lets the "trash be honoured as the quick". The way out of this impasse is by faith—faith in oneself to discover the real.

The last six lines present a typical young man's conclusion. 'All is not lost', the poet insists. 'We shall not be hoodwinked by the past and its ghosts; but through endurance and fortitude shall become "fit fellows for a life".' A rather unusual degree of optimism for Thomas to voice.

The coincidence of the processes of love and destruction appear in a number of Thomas' poems. *When, like a running grave* seems to take for its theme the simultaneous workings of love (a creative force) and time (a destructive one). Thus, when we look on the performance of love, we are likewise looking upon death: "a turtle in a hearse". And the agent of love (the male organ) becomes "Cadaver's shoot of bud of Adam" and "Cadaver's candle". Similarly, the female partner ("Your calm and cuddled") becomes the instrument of death ("a scythe of hairs", suggestive both of the motion of intercourse and of the curve of the female genitals).

Time as "a running grave" is also a memorable phrase, substituting as it does for the movement of man towards his death the movement of his death towards him. When, as in this instance, Thomas' poems do not come off, we are left with two or three brilliant *disjecta membra*, the unassembled limbs of an inchoate composition.

The synchronised activity of the powers of love and destruction is the theme of that much-anthologised piece, *The force that through the green fuse drives the flower*. The poem posits the oneness of man and nature, and the unity of the world in a creative-destructive continuum.

> The force that through the green fuse drives the flower
> Drives my green age; that blasts the roots of trees
> Is my destroyer.

In reading Thomas' poem, I find myself reminded of

Blake's *The Sick Rose*. In both cases we get the idea of physical beauty preyed on by a destructive force; but there is more than the thought of destruction present.[13] Both poems show the destructive force as associated with a creative energy. By Thomas' act of juxta-position, we are made to feel that the "wintry fever" is only another mode of "The force that through the green fuse drives the flower". Similarly, in Blake's poem "the invisible worm" which destroys the rose finds in that destruction "his dark secret love".

The first stanza insists that the forces in nature which work for growth and destruction work for growth and destruction in the poet. Man and nature are co-extensive.

From the statement of this cosmic proposition, the poet passes on, in stanza three, to consider the behaviour of energy in the form of sexual love (its chief manifestation in the human realm, he appears to believe):

> Love drips and gathers, but the fallen blood
> Shall calm her sores.

[13] The rose has, from primitive times, been the symbol of the female genitals; and Blake seems also to have used flower-images to represent the generative organs of both sexes (as in *Ah! Sun-flower*, where among other things, the flower stands for the male member). *The Sick Rose* seems to me a poetic "parable" on feminine masturbation. I will give the trains-of-thought that lead to such a reading.

The "dark secret love" of "the invisible worm" destroys the rose's life. But if the worm, which has found out the flower's "bed of crimson joy" represents the phallus, so that the poem is seen to be speaking about love between the sexes, why should the rose be destroyed by such love? Then, too, the worm is spoken of as "invisible"—another factor which strengthens my interpretation. We note also that the climate of the worm is one suggestive of grief and destruction: it flies in "the howling storm".

It can be maintained, of course, that only a literal reading of the poem is acceptable; but this would ignore the "parable method" so often present in Blake's *Songs of Experience* (*The Garden of Love*, *A Poison Tree*, *A Little Boy Lost*, *The Clod and the Pebble*), as well as the strange vividness of the poem, which is best described, I think, by the word erotic. As I have already suggested Thomas' early vision of sex is very largely onanistic. Whether or not his words refer to such forms of sexual practice, or whether they speak of normal intercourse, the accent tends to fall upon waste and dispersal of energy. The two poems, then, Blake's and Thomas', have a theme of destruction in common.

"Love drips and gathers" is a statement applicable to both the sexes. What is important to note is that love's "sore" is only to be calmed by "the fallen blood" (an image of sacrifice and dispersal). It is possible to interpret this passage in greater sexual detail: love's "sore" may be read as the open womb, "sore" because of menstruation, and "sore" also in a psychological sense (which we may indicate by the words 'annoyed', 'frustrated') because it has been balked of its proper function of conception. "The fallen blood" of the male seed calms this aggravated condition, since by impregnation the "sores" are healed.

The poem ends on a note of dismay:

And I am dumb to tell the lover's tomb
How at my sheet goes the same crooked worm.

The end of love, as Thomas sees it in these early poems, is not fertility but death. To the image of implied fruitfulness in the third stanza succeed these images of destruction. The lover's final resting-place is not the bed but the tomb; and "the worm", which sometimes features as the organ of creation becomes here the insect of destruction. And it is peculiarly the lover's worm also.

A more dynamic account—though not so successful poetically—of the 'pantheistic' relations between man and nature is given in the poem *All all and the dry world's lever*. Sex, or a process analogous to it, a process of dynamic attraction, is, the poet feels, the "lever" of the world, without which things would be "dry" (and separated). Everything, then, issues forth from "the oil, the pound of lava" (an image of the male seed and the womb's ova); so that the world can be said to be "all of the flesh", in just the same way as the poet's "naked fellow" (the male member) is one with the "Dug of the sea" and the "Worm in the scalp".

The second section of the poem is an argument of self-assurance. The poet is exhorting himself not to fear the act of sex ("the tread, the seeded milling", "Nor the flint in the lover's mauling") since these are one with the processes which determine and sustain "the working world".

Section three re-states the catholicity of the law of attraction: "All all and all the dry worlds couple"; but the last stanza is weakened for me by an adscititious political reference: "Flower, flower the people's fusion", which reads rather like the vague and lyrical Communism that Stephen Spender once dealt in. Indeed, it was difficult for a poet of that time (1934)[14] to avoid the more colourful clichés of the Left, even for a poet as subjective and introspective as Thomas. This is one of his few political references, and is clearly no contribution to the thought of the poem.

There are, however, valid images in the last stanza: the lovely "coupled bud" (amplified into "the spun bud of the world", in a later poem *A Winter's Tale*), "the drive of oil", "the brassy blood". But the last line has no tautness, and its repetition achieves only the 'pseudo-intense'.

The greater part of Thomas' early poetic thought is summarised in the poem *Light breaks where no sun shines*. Here, we find his 'pantheism'; his sense that "One thought fills immensity" (as Blake expressed it in his *Proverbs of Hell*); his feeling for the identity of opposites (indicated even in the paradoxical wording of the title), and his 'biological' explanation of the universe.

As Marshall W. Stearns has analysed this poem, at some length (pp. 14–18 of his pamphlet *Unsex the Skeleton*, and, in slighter shorter form, as an appendix to Henry Treece's book on the poet), I shall not under-

---

[14] For a more mature and responsible social-political comment, we have to wait for *The hand that signed the paper* in *25 Poems*.

take to examine it again. "Of the various lev
meaning it communicates", he writes, "I take i
the basic level is a description of the state of exist
the theme is the process of living." With his state
and account I substantially agree.

25 Poems

I

PUBLISHED IN 1936, *25 Poems* is chiefly remarkable for the strong discrepancy of style in its constituent pieces. It contains both poems more involved and simple than the simplest or the most difficult in the previous collection. Henry Treece has referred to Thomas, in one aspect of his creative role, as a "straight poet", and there are at least six poems in this volume which have the signature of a "straight poet" upon them. These poems are also the best in the book, and when I call them "straight" pieces, I am speaking comparatively, from within the body of Thomas' verse. They have not the 'straightness' which we might expect from W. H. Davies or Walter de la Mare, but they are no more difficult that many poems by T. S. Eliot, or W. H. Auden, or the early C. Day Lewis. These poems, which I shall examine later, are: *Why east wind chills, This bread I break, Ears in the turret hear, I have longed to move away, The hand that signed the paper, And death shall have no dominion.* Relatively simple, also, is the poem *Shall gods be said to thump the clouds*—a partly playful denial of the anthropomorphic notion of the gods: "It shall be said that gods are stone", and that the stones do not speak. It is hardly, however, a memorable piece.

But if the above pieces possess the strength of the best work in *18 Poems*, there are many which are more involved and chaotic. *I, in my intricate image, Foster the*

64

light, Grief thief of time, How soon the servant sun, together
with the ten 'sonnets' of *Altarwise by owl-light* have
no consistency of image or image-group; and, save
for one specimen piece, I shall not try to interpret
them. To me, they seem to show the seething unrest
of the transition period. The "foetal unity" and sex-
preoccupation of the *18 Poems* is varied and mingled
with other themes here; and, on the whole, I can detect
no sign of a satisfying synthesis.

There are traces of doubt, questioning, and despair
in many of these pieces. *Was there a time* deals with the
corruption of innocence by experience, and the
murdering of hope by the passage of time. Indeed,
one must not be misled by the vigour and excitement
of Thomas' early poetry into thinking that he is an
optimistic poet. His poetic temperament has a dark
facet to it, and the thoughts in his earlier compositions
are often pessimistic. For instance, his statement that,

> What's never known is safest in this life.

parallels Auden's line that "Not to be born is the
best for man".

A general spirit of inquiry, frustrated by a sense of
irony or cynicism, seems to pervade *25 Poems*. In the
third stanza of *Should lanterns shine*, the poet comments
upon all the didactic teaching he has had, and just how
far it has benefitted him:

> I have heard many years of telling,
> And many years should see some change.

The remark is non-commital, but we feel the scepticism
of its tone. The poet sees only futility in striving to
solve his own problems by the methods of traditional
moral codes. We are reminded of Omar Khyyam who
had "heard great argument" when young, yet, finally
and inescapably, "came out from that same door

wherein [he] went". *Should lanterns shine* does, in fact, present us with one of the dilemmas which Thomas was facing:

> I have been told to reason by the heart,
> But heart, like head, leads hopelessly.

Neither in conventional morality, nor in more 'emancipated' ethics, is he able to find a principle of conduct.

In one poem *Incarnate devil* the suggestion seems to be that evil and deathliness entered the world with the knowledge of what we call good and evil:

> The wisemen tell me that the garden gods
> Twined good and evil on an eastern tree;
> And when the moon rose windily it was
> Black as the beast and paler than the cross.

What we get here is a variation on the Garden of Eden story; but, typically enough, the idea of disobedience has been omitted. According to Thomas' myth, it was not an action (Eve's picking of the apple) which changed affairs, but the introduction of a conception (of good and evil behaviour). His myth appears to pre-suppose a pristine state of unthinking goodness, a Golden Age when man acted rightly without reflection or consciousness of it. (Something of this hard-dying fancy of a Golden Age is present in one of his last poems *In country sleep*. See, particularly, the fifth and sixth stanzas in section one, and such lines as "The country is holy: O bide in that country kind,".). The extirpation of an elemental and pre-ethical innocence is reflected likewise in the words of another poem, "this/Murder of Eden and green genesis."

But the indecisiveness of the poet's position, in which he is morally neither here nor there, is most fully presented in the poem *I have longed to move away*. For the Christian interpretation of things, Thomas admits to both repulsion and attraction; and although, intellectually, he feels such religion to be only "the hissing of the spent lie", with another part of himself he is less certain about denying it:

> I have longed to move away but am afraid;
> Some life, yet unspent, might explode
> Out of the old lie burning on the ground,
> And, crackling in the air, leave me half-blind.

Until we come to the 'sonnet'-sequence *Altarwise by owl-light* which concludes the book, there is no consistency of tone or approach; nor anything like a tendency to a solution. Moods of rebellion and acceptance follow hard upon one another's heels, as in the poem *Find meat on bones*:

> Rebel against the binding moon
> And the parliament of sky,

which, in turn, forces from the poet the admission:

> I cannot murder, like a fool,
> Season and sunshine, grace and girl,
> Nor can I smother the sweet waking.

But a rage against "the sky [which] lays down her laws" gathers again in the poet, even though he is led to understand that

> Light and dark are no enemies
> But one companion.

So he resumes his anathema:

> War on the destiny of man!
> Doom on the sun!

Suddenly, as if he had been frightened by his cursing, or received some abrupt access of revelation, he ends the poem with the words,

> Before death takes you, O take back this.

Is it fear or humility in face of the universe? We cannot say, but may find ourselves reminded of Rimbaud's plea from *A Season in Hell*, "Slaves, let us not curse existence." Man cannot live in rebellion, as Dostoievsky's character so truly remarked; but, despite this particular conclusion, Thomas in *25 Poems* is far from making his general peace.

The main troubling factor in the thought of this book is the introduction of religious ideas (of a semi-Christian order) to a greater degree than in *18 Poems*. Whereas the chief preoccupations in this last volume were the physical and cosmic attributes of sex, referring to the intercourse between man and woman, and mankind's relationship with the universe, in *25 Poems* we have the attempt, in a dark and tentative fashion, to view life as much in religious, as in sexual terms.

It is true that there are still references to the 'pantheistic' view of life which permeated *18 Poems*, as in *This bread I break* and *The seed-at-zero*. In the latter of these pieces, the poet gives an imaginative account of the kind of continuity and consummation we may expect at death. "The seed-at-zero" which, we are told, shall not storm "the trodden womb", represents man with his vital forces spent; man, in other words, in a condition of death. Man's goal, the poet implies, is not, ultimately, the womb of woman but the womb of the universe:

> Through the ramparts of the sky
> Shall the star-flecked seed be riddled,[1]

It is the 'pantheistic' conception of the dispersal of

---

[1] Compare this description of sublimated sexual energies in death with the description of the sublimation of sexual forces in old age, in the poem *Light breaks where no sun shines:*
> Where no seed stirs
> The fruit of man unwrinkles in the stars.

man's being at death among the other forces of nature, which are really one with his own:

> Manna for the guarded ground,
> Quickening for the virgin sea;

But it is the powerful entry of Christian currents of thought that create new and warring elements in these poems. This tendency reaches full expression in the 'sonnets' of *Altarwise by owl-light*, where the poet strives to incorporate his view of sex in a religious context.

I do not consider this 'sonnet'- sequence to be successful poetically. Its imagery appears as the nearest thing to an extended mixed metaphor imaginable, and its tone violent, forced, and histrionic. But whether or not I am right in my judgment, the importance of these poems as having a place in Thomas' thought is not inconsiderable. In his book *Auden and After*, Francis Scarfe has ingeniously unravelled the meaning of the sequence (pp. 106–110); and of 'sonnet' eight (a crucifixion piece) he writes, "In a sense the poem seems to symbolise the birth of love through the death of sex. Mary suffers the true punishment of Eve —not merely the pangs of child-birth, but the death of her offspring. The full symbolism only appears towards the end of the poem, with the words "Unsex the skeleton this mountain minute". . . . The conclusion to be drawn from this fine crucifixion poem is disturbing. After presenting in all his poems a brilliant sexual interpretation of life, Dylan Thomas has here presented a sexual interpretation of death. The secret of death, and its horror, is that it is sexless."[2]

II

The pressure of contending spiritual loyalties, of the

---

[2] It is interesting to compare this interpretation with that of Marshall W. Stearns in his pamphlet *Unsex the Skeleton* (pp. 9–12).

pull or repulsion of certain ideas, is reflected in the style of *25 Poems*. This reflection is no direct matter, expressing itself in any terms of recognisable opposites, but is present in a close-knit darkness of style. The strain of attempting to embrace antitheses, or of living with ideas with which he has no proper understanding, seems to have muddled the poet in Thomas.

In so far as we can say (after subtracting the six or seven "straight" poems) that the book possesses a norm of expression, this norm proves often an unfathomable mirror:

> And father all nor fail the fly-lord's acre,
> Nor sprout on owl-seed like a goblin-sucker,
> But rail with your wizard's ribs the heart-shaped planet;

Henry Treece has made the point that Thomas was not beyond compounding "a poetic leg-pull". This may well be so; but I do not think it applies to many of the obscurities we encounter in *25 Poems*. These, I think, are the product of a mind whose imagination was so far ahead of its intelligence that sometimes the latter was out-stripped completely. It is then that we get, not light but darkness—a poetic darkness, if you will; but one, in Henry Treece's words, which "it is a waste of time to decipher." For, as he frankly observes, "one must draw the line somewhere."

As an organic sequence, or as a body of verse judged on its general level, *25 Poems* is not satisfactory. Out of the contents of twenty-four pieces, plus the ten 'sonnets' of *Altarwise by owl-light*, I would extract only half a dozen which are worthy of long consideration, and in which the power of conveying pleasure does not stem from 'cross-word' satisfaction but from the recognition of genuine poetic attributes. Before turning to a commentary on these, I should like to attempt an analysis of one of the 'difficult' poems. My choice is the first one in the book, *I, in my intricate image*.

One theme of the poem would appear to be the double existence that man leads: on the levels of the flesh and of the spirit. The first is probably represented by the image of "the brassy orator" (Brass is not one of the precious metals, and, with its connotation of 'bold' and 'hard' as applying to human character, is an adjective to suggest the material claims of the human make-up. Further, the image of "the brassy orator" carries other nuances of meaning: one dealing in hard and factual arguments, one who makes no appeal to sentiment—'hard as brass' is a proverbial description of a certain type of character—and one who speaks almost mechanically without the usual human motivations—a sort of robot-man.)

The other side of the poet's nature is reflected in the image of "my half ghost in armour" (indicative of the spirit, housed, yet also imprisoned, in the flesh's corporeal shell).

There are also the usual references to the male and female parts (the conflict and tension between the sexes appearing as a parallel to the conflict and tension between flesh and spirit in the individual being). Thus, the phallic "steeplejack tower, bonerailed and master-less" is off-set by the vaginal "corkscrew grave centred in navel and nipple".

There is, too, some talk of "a double image" which might well stand for a figure of fusion, of hard-won unity; but the whole poem is so full of discrepant and disparate images that no one conclusion seems arrived at.

Another theme would appear to be that of "The natural parallel"—of the way in which non-human existence reduplicates the behaviour of human living; but it is difficult to see this analogy actually developing in the lines before us. The following three stanzas,

for example, seem to speak of the conception of a
child and its delivery at birth, but when we ask for
detail or exactness the interpretation becomes inadequate:

> Be by your one ghost pierced, his pointed ferrule,
> Brass and the bodiless image, on a stick of folly
> Star-set at Jacob's angle,
> Smoke hill and hophead's valley,
> And the five-fathomed Hamlet on his father's coral,
> Thrusting the tom-thumb vision up the iron mile.
>
> Suffer the slash of vision by the fin-green stubble,
> Be by the ships' sea broken at the manstring anchored
> The stoved bones' voyage downward
> In the shipwreck of muscle;
> Give over, lovers, locking, and the seawax struggle,
> Love like a mist or fire through the bed of eels.
>
> And in the pincers of the boiling circle,
> The sea and instrument, nicked in the locks of time,
> My great blood's iron single
> In the pouring town,
> I, in a wind on fire, from green Adam's cradle,
> No man more magical, clawed out the crocodile.

Now it would be easy enough to force a meaning
into these lines from without, but to take them as they
stand and extract a meaning *from* them is an altogether
different matter. There is too great a distance between
image and image, too vast a conjectural space between
noun and adjective, for the mind to span. The "pincers
of the boiling circle" (a gynaecological instrument?) is
an example of this. It is hard to obtain a visual picture
of this image; and, if at length, we do so (seeing a
circular furrow round which boiling water moves to
meet itself at the starting-point), we are still far from
its relevance or meaning.

"And my images roared and rose on heaven's hill"
concludes the poet. So be it: heaven may understand
him, I do not.

III

It is as if all the half-frustrated thought which muddies and thickens *25 Poems* sought, and sought successfully, an egress in some half-dozen pieces. Perhaps they are the result of forces that verbally broke through some mental inhibition because of their single-mindedness, the assertive clarity of their content. Most of them, indeed, say something definite, something more single in import, than any of Thomas' previous poems.

Some of these poems are religious in nature, but in a 'pantheistic' or metaphysical sense. The question of sin and guilt (present in the 'sonnet'-sequence) is found here only in one of them—the autobiographical statement, *I have longed to move away*.

Of these half-dozen pieces, the two chief religious poems are *This bread I break*, *And death shall have no dominion*. Inspired by Thomas' 'sacramental' view of life, the first of these is one of his most compact poems, its theme being the oneness of man's life with nature. Thus, when the poet eats a piece of bread, he does it 'in remembrance of' "the oat" from which it was made. The wine he drinks seems to have come direct from "a foreign tree", upon which the fruit that yielded it once hung. And in order that the oat should become bread, and the fruit become wine, sacrifice was necessary:

> Man in the day or wind at night
> Laid the crops low, broke the grape's joy.[3]

In fact, as the poem continues we see that Thomas is describing here a sort of 'pantheistic' eucharist. In the second stanza, while still pendant on the tree, the

[3] Marshall W. Stearns interprets this poem differently. Thomas, he maintains, "twists the traditional symbolism of communion into far different channels, saying that man destroys himself by utilizing the grape and the oat to make wine and bread."

fruit becomes "flesh" and its juice becomes "blood":

> Once in this wind the summer blood
> Knocked in the flesh that decked the vine,

and again the stanza ends with the notion of destruction—a sort of sacrificial process, necessary to human
preservation and creation. And in this last line—
"Man broke the sun, pulled the wind down"—we have
another example of that mode of thinking by trans-
ference, which the poet so often employed. Actually,
of course, it is not "the sun" and "the wind" which
man pulls down when he plucks the grapes, but the
workings of these within the fruits.

The last stanza contains what may be termed a
'pantheistic' counter-part to the Catholic attitude to the
Mass. Just as the first line of the first stanza suggests
the Gospel passage, "this do in remembrance of me"
(*St. Luke* 22, verse 9) so the last line of the last stanza
recalls Christ's other statement, as reported by the
Apostle, on the occasion of the Last Supper, "This
is my body which is given for you" (or, according to
St. Matthew, "Take, eat; this is my body".);

> This flesh you break, this blood you let
> Make desolation in the vein,
> Were oat and grape
> Born of the sensual root and sap;
> My wine you drink, my bread you snap.

Sacrifice or a giving to others, in a process destructive
to the object or the self, is the theme of the stanza,
which the last line clinches. This time it is sacrifice
through the act of love. The poet tells his mistress
that in their union she drinks his wine and eats his
bread (as this is an out-going energy it leaves a
"desolation in the vein"). And this vital force be-
queathed in sexual love is "Born of the sensual root
and sap": the oat that was "merry in the wind", and

the wine that was "Plunged in its fruit". So the act of sacrifice (seeming in part an act of destruction) has involved both nature and man (whose act, in turn, implicates woman through the partly self-destructive sacrifice of child-bearing).

Just as the last poem asserted the continuity of life through sacrifice, so the following piece asserts the continuity of life after death. *And death shall have no dominion* deals with the theme of resurrection; and it is probable that the rumours of many sermons, in the poet's 'Biblical' native land, contributed to its composition.

St. Paul's first epistle to the Corinthians abounds in texts that are often quoted. "For since by man *came* death", writes the Apostle, "by man also *came* the resurrection of the dead" (verse 21). "For as in Adam all die, even so in Christ shall all be made alive" (verse 22). This is the theme of *Corinthians 15*; and— without the implicit reference to divine power—such is the theme of the poem. But its spirit is better apprehended by comparing it with the most exalted passages in the fifteenth chapter of St. Paul's *Epistle* verses 51– 55: "Behold, I shew you a mystery; We shall not all sleep, but we shall all be changed/In a moment, in the twinkling of an eye, at the last trump: for the trumpet shall sound, and the dead shall be raised incorruptible, and we shall be changed./For this corruptible must put on incorruption, and this mortal *must* put on immortality./So when this corruptible shall have put on incorruption, and this mortal shall have put on immortality, then shall be brought to pass the saying that is written, Death is swallowed up in victory./O death, where *is* thy sting? O grave, where *is* thy victory?"

With like fervour the poet celebrates the continuance of living, which he feels not even death can disrupt. But concerning the mode of resurrection, Thomas and St. Paul differ. For the Apostle, there can be no question of man's natural body being retained ("Now this I say, brethren, that flesh and blood cannot inherit the kingdom of God", verse 50). According to him, the being of man is created or "sown a natural body" but "it is raised a spiritual body. There is a natural body and there is a spiritual body" (verse 44).

To Thomas, this distinction does not apply. For him, "the natural body" is something less limited than for the Apostle. He sees it as persisting through the changes of death; persisting, that is, as an atom of vitality, though it loses its original constitution. So, in the last stanza, the poet writes that

> Heads of the characters hammer through daisies;

The life in the individual endures, though with death it changes its mode of existence: the energy of life passes from the body of a person to nourish a wild flower. This is a further example of the poet's 'pantheism'.

A tribute to the persistence of the life-force, this is one of Thomas' noblest pieces. It is simple in structure, having three nine-line stanzas, each of them beginning and ending with the *motif* of the composition, "And death shall have no dominion". The development of the poem is by repetition. Nothing is added which carries us beyond the first statement, but, by various examples, the statement is imaginatively amplified.

The first stanza contains a very beautiful play upon the colloquial image of "the man in the moon". To this familiar phrase, the poet has added the thought of the west wind; and from their combination produced the strange and exquisite line: "the man in the wind and the west moon". There is also an entrancing and delicate repetition in the third line of this stanza—

"When their bones are picked clean and the clean bones gone"—which may remind us of the resurrection

of the dry bones in the thirty-seventh chapter of
Ezekiel, or T. S. Eliot's images of bones in *Ash-Wednesday*; and which, from a literary stand-point,
compares favourably with either.

The third of the religious poems, among the six best
pieces from this book, is less decisive than the previous
two. There is a strong will to rejection in it, but this
will is balanced by a sort of hesitating half-belief.
Some critics have interpreted it as the poet's effort to
dismiss the nonconformist moral background; but I
think it is more likely a denial of convention rather
than of genuine religion. In it, church-going and convention are equated; and the last lines of the poem
make it clear what the real object of opposition is:
"Half convention and half lie".

> the old terror's continual cry
> Growing more terrible as the day
> Goes over the hill into the deep sea;

may refer to the hell-fire sermons preached at evening
service in some of the Welsh chapels, or it may refer
to a persisting sense of guilt and foreboding descend-
ing on the poet at each day's close.

I think the first interpretation is the more probable;
as the words which speak of it are followed by a
mention of other conventions and formalities which
the poet wishes to avoid ("the repetition of salutes",
"the parting of hat from hair"—hand-shakes and
raising of the hat).

The substance of the poem seems to be, that religion
—for the poet—is a matter of fiction, as polite and
'meaningless' as raising one's hat; but that he is afraid
to renounce it utterly for fear that some part of it is
still valid.

Yet if there is some truth ("some life") in this
religious orthodoxy, the poet would prefer to die
outside of it; since it appears of so mixed a nature:

> By these I would not care to die,
> Half convention and half lie.

But along with the repudiation of cant and religiosity, the poem satirizes and rejects the prim middle-class way of behaviour. "Pursed lips at the receiver" refers, I imagine, to the purely conventional kisses with which returning husbands greet, and are greeted by, their wives.

Why east wind chills is one of Thomas' finest and most lyrical pieces. Drenched in a mood of sombre mystery, the poem must be read as an agnostic's confession. But it is the confession of an agnostic who does not wish to argue over his position. His agnosticism is really a homage or compliment to the profundity of existence (such a tribute as Nietzsche paid when he wrote that "The world is deep, and deeper than the day thinks it").

The starting-off point of the poem is the asking of questions which can never be answered. Like a child, the poet wants to know why things, which are "not otherwise but thus", should be so; and in what lies their first cause. But to his enquiries,

> Why east wind chills and south wind cools
>   .   .   .   .
> Why silk is soft and the stone wounds

the poet tells us "He'll have a black reply". In other words, the answer will be negative; that is, it will be no answer, or one shrouded in the blackness of mystery.

The next stanza develops the analogy between the child-like questioning poet and the instinctive enquiring child:

> When cometh Jack Frost? the children ask.

By using the old form of the verb ("cometh"), the poet suggests the historic past through which children

have asked the same question. The archaic form uni-
versalizes the sentence. And, again, the unanswerable
nature of things is the only answer they can receive.
This time it is suggested by a number of subtle images
The exact predictability of the frost is something as
difficult to determine as it is to "clasp a comet" in
one's fist. Both frost in its cold and the comet in its
heat are refined elements, almost impalpable. The
juxtaposition of chill and fiery substances, in the
parallel of "frost" and "comet", is the more effective
in that they possess one common quality: a shining
whiteness. And if we can imagine a child holding a
portion of a comet in its hand, the appearance would
be similar to that of a child holding a frosted icicle.

The last four lines of the stanza are a little involved.
Just as the archaic employment of "cometh" took us
back into the past, so these four lines carry us into the
future—a future infinitely remote. No "white answer",
the poet tells us, will "echo from the rooftops", until
the dust of the questioning children

> Sprinkles in children's eyes a long-last sleep
> And dusk is crowded with the children's ghosts,

There can be no answer until death: until after the
death of the children who put the question, and the
death of these children's children.

With the third stanza, the resignation—which in the
first two was filled with pathos—becomes informed
with a kind of wisdom. "All things are known", the
poet begins, with the suggestion of omniscience
present in heaven if not attainable on earth. But the
advice of the stars, as they "round" "the towers of the
sky", is to " 'Be content' ". The words of the stars are
like the music of the spheres, and in their words is
celestial wisdom. This wisdom is little heard by men,
but the poet hears it, and though it is only a gentle
admonition to "Rest in the riddle" (as the hero

counsels in Christopher Fry's play *The Lady's not for Burning*), his acceptance of it leaves him more serene. The admonitory note in the words " 'Be content' " is emphasised by the image of "a handbell through the corridor" (a school reference), which is how the heavenly message sounds to the poet. But there are still under-tones of sadness in this resignation; and the idea of a handbell ringing the children back to class has a partly melancholy sound for one whose school-days will not return. This sadness at the heart of things is brought out by the transient and unsubstantial images in the last lines: "ghostly comets", "man of frost", and "echo's answer".

The unknowable and incommunicable nature of the universe, which was the subject of the last poem, is matched by another which deals with the incommunicable nature of the self. *Ears in the turret hear* is a poem on the isolation of the individual sealed in the unshareable nature of his own being. The poet describes the isolated spirit in the figure of a tower (a building which rejects the forces of the besieging world). In a similar way, W. B. Yeats uses the image of a tower in his poem *Blood and the Moon* to suggest isolated superiority. The tower in Thomas' poem is essentially an image of isolation, rather in the manner of the philosopher Leibniz's conception of the "windowless monad".

It might be helpful to compare the poem with *This bread I break*, which posits the community of all created matter. In contrast to this, *Ears in the turret hear* springs from a mood of utter incommunicability, of a suspicion and fear of life. But the urge to seek and retain this isolation is balanced by the burden of loneliness; so that from the tension develops this question:

> Shall I unbolt or stay
> Alone till the day I die

In the solitude of his selfhood, the poet hears "Hands grumble at the door"; and, watching from the turret of his tower, listens to "The fingers at the locks". Shall he unbolt, or shall he stay: this is the question the poet asks himself?

But before he reaches a decision, he would like to know what the outside world, represented by the abstract "hands", has to offer; namely, whether "poison or grapes".

As with many of Thomas' poems, there is no real development and no conclusion. The dilemma is voiced, with varied imagery through three stanzas, and left largely in the state in which the poet first expressed it.

The hand that signed the paper is the most objective and historically-minded of Thomas' "straight" pieces. But although the subjective references, so typical of the poet, are lacking in this poem, it retains the same vision as the personal pieces. This vision I would describe as a highly intuitive sense of the continuity of time and place—the power of seeing an object or an action in all its states or tenses of time. Future and present—usually removed from each other in our mind—are telescoped and juxtaposed by Thomas, as when he writes of an action and its consequence in the one compressed line:

> The hand that signed the paper felled a city;

Through this device of vision the poet makes cause and effect abut upon each other with a sharp realisation.

The whole poem is remarkable for its cinematic technique:

> The hand that signed the paper felled a city;
> Five sovereign fingers taxed the breath,
> Doubled the globe of dead and halved a country;
> These five kings did a king to death.

Throughout it, the fingers of the politician's hand are granted "sovereign" importance, on account of the power they wield through the pen. The sovereign powers of the politician are shown as vested in the fingers alone: with these he signs decisive documents, but, for the rest of the man, there is nothing kingly or impressive about him ("The mighty hand leads to a sloping shoulder,/The finger joints are cramped with chalk").

In a quick series of photo-flashes, as at a film, we see the hand signing the fatal paper which will lead to war erupting across a continent. Film-like too, the activating hand is shown impersonally, without a head attached, so that the inhuman aspect of the action becomes the more evident. Next, the results of this action—the processes of war and famine—follow the first image without intermission. And what is the sum of it all?—

> The five kings count the dead but do not soften
> The crusted wound nor stroke the brow;
> A hand rules pity as a hand rules heaven;
> Hands have no tears to flow.

Pity, that complex sentiment, is reduced to the mathematical and mechanical level of a straight line. The hands of a politician are like levers, not human members in contact with a heart:

> Hands have no tears to flow.

The Map of Love

I

PUBLISHED IN 1939, *The Map of Love* consisted of sixteen poems and seven tales in prose.[1] Hastily regarded, the volume gives the impression of a variety new to the poet, which has been obtained at the cost of a central mood or theme. Unlike Thomas' two previous books of verse, *The Map of Love* lacks the sense of imaginative relationship. It is more of a personal miscellany.

Henry Treece has well summarised the most important elements in these poems. "They deal," he writes,[2] "variously with the poet's description of his beloved (*I make this in a warring absence.* . . .), his announcement that he has received the call of 'religion' (*It is the sinners' dust-tongued bells claps me to churches*), his grief at the death of an old lady (*In Memory of Ann Jones*), and his moralising on the fact that he has written little for some time (*On no work of words now for three lean months*), his greetings to his unborn child (*A Saint about to fall*), a conversation between an unborn child and its mother-to-be (*If my head hurts a hair's foot*), and that final poem of this section (*Twenty-four years remind the tears of my eyes*), in which the poet bewails an unheroic future."[3]

[1] I have dealt with the prose section of *The Map of Love* in Part Three, Prose and Drama, chapter one—Prose.
[2] *Dylan Thomas* (1949).
[3] Henry Treece refers to the original titles of the poems, as they appeared in *The Map of Love*. In *Collected Poems* there are some slight changes.

Sound, too, is the conclusion which he draws from this list of subject-matters. "There is," he remarks, "as is apparent even from this crude analysis, a widening of Thomas' interests. They even admit the separate existence of others beside the poet, in the persons of Ann Jones and the unborn child."

But what is most interesting in *The Map of Love* is the way in which the poet speaks of these other beings. Hitherto, his chief method has been to identify himself with others by using their voice, by speaking through their person—a kind of ventriloquist poetry. So, in *18 Poems*, the poet speaks through the unborn child or through the seed of its future father. This method is continued in *The Map of Love*, but the parties and their vantage-points are largely new. The voice or *persona* of the child or the man were those most common to Thomas' first books. Now, in the poem *How shall my animal*, we have the utterance of femininity, of woman's apprehension and knowledge of the male in the act of physical union.

The images in this poem are confused, as if they came from a host of hesitating and contradictory feelings. But there is one lovely and lasting image of the lovers in the act of love. The woman is shown as a mare, "trotting" "with a loud mate the haybeds of a mile". Of recent equine imagery employed to describe physical union, this, I think, is the very best. Alex Comfort's image of the partners, in his poem *The Postures of Love*, seems both diffused and remote beside it:

> This was Octavia's way, the rider's way
> straight like a candle, her hair a flame,
> and outstretched Anthony saw in her half-light
> her white horse galloping beside his own.

The unborn child has always played a prominent role in Thomas' poetry; but its words have generally been addressed to the world at large. Here, in *If my head hurts a hair's foot*, the child directly addresses its mother, and the mother replies. What we get in this conversation is an added focus and particularity. The situation becomes specific; and is interpreted in dramatic rather than cosmological terms.

But there are serious flaws in the poem. As Henry Treece has observed, there is a "humourless plethora of sound and deafness" in the lines,

> If the unpricked ball of my breath
> Bump on a spout let the bubbles jump out.

The occasion calls for intimacy of tone, for a quiet or tender voice; or for the rhetoric of vibrant life. Least of all does it demand the verbal *tour-de-force* or variety-act with consonants and vowels, which we are given.

Then, abruptly, in the third stanza, the slap-stick language disappears:

> If my bunched, monkey coming is cruel
> Rage me back to the making house.

the child tremendously urges its mother. The rest of the stanza, however, cannot keep pace with this forceful expressiveness.

The mother's reply, which follows next, occupies the rest of the poem. The voice is passionate, and through this passion is able to sustain its grandiloquence of speech:

> 'No. Not for Christ's dazzling bed
> Or a nacreous sleep among soft particles and charms
> My dear would I change my tears or your iron head.

The next stanza also contains expressive lines, where the originality of statement is still sufficiently suffused with feeling as not to appear artificially novel.

> O my lost love bounced from a good home;

is how the mother refers to the child delivered from her womb.

The poem is far too uneven to be considered a success. Its importance lies in the more exact and individual depiction which it bestows on the theme of birth. In keeping closer to the particular, the composition gains dramatic qualities which the universal treatment of the theme in Thomas' earlier poetry lacked.

But in the finest poem in *The Map of Love* the poet does not merge his voice in that of the subject. *After the funeral (In memory of Ann Jones)* is a triumph of poetic sympathy, not through identification but through objective perception.

After the funeral is a poem of love; and it is the more unusual in that its heroine, poor seventy-year-old Ann, is so uncomely a figure:

> I know her scrubbed and sour humble hands
> Lie with religion in their cramp, her threadbare
> Whisper in a damp word, her wits drilled hollow,
> Her fist of a face died clenced on a round pain;

It is hardly a flattering account the poet gives. "Scrubbed", "sour", and "fist" are parsimonious terms; and "damp" is so weak and neutral in impact as to suggest something mildly repulsive.

Against this, we have the ambiguous word "religion" in the phrase concerning Ann's hands, which "Lie with religion in their cramp". This can be interpreted both positively or negatively. We can take it as a synonym for 'patience'; so that the passage means, 'In their condition of cramp, her hands rest resignedly'. Or we can take "religion "to suggest the sclerotic accretions of conventional worship; so that the poet's meaning is, 'Ann's hands are as cramped as her stiff religious notions'. It seems to me quite

probable that the poet had both meanings in mind:
justice to the claims of unlovely truth and love.

However we receive the passage, the next line exalts
and magnifies the status of this little old woman:

And sculptured Ann is seventy years of stone.

In this classical line all the pettinesses of poor Ann
Jones appear smoothed out, fancifully—we may say—
as death smooths out the puckers in her face.

And with this restitution of her image, the background to her life is rehabilitated also. The desiccated
lower-middle-class existence, evoked by a room with
a stuffed fox and a stale fern, is dismissed and cancelled
out by the change which overcomes these background
'properties'. Devoid of love and devoid of grace, these
images—through the poet's ceremony of remembrance
—are suddenly and miraculously transformed, so that
"The stuffed lung of the fox [twitches and cries] Love/
And the strutting fern [lays] seeds on the black sill."

This technique of transformation may recall the
use which Baudelaire makes of it in his terrible poem
Les Métamorphoses du Vampire. But with the French
poet the imaginative change is one in an opposite
direction—from beauty to horror—and not, as in
Thomas' poem, from the banal to the beautiful. The
woman with "sa bouche de fraise" becomes "une
outre aux flancs gluants, toute pleine de pus"; and,
later still, "des débris de squelette".

The process of Thomas' transformation-scene is
analagous, also, to Nietzsche's "transvaluation of
values". In both cases, our imaginative notion
of the world is altered; but whereas Nietzsche deals
in the alchemy of ideas, Thomas is concerned with that
of images, by which the barren mundane outline of
some object is poetically resolved into pure gold.

The only other poem in *The Map of Love* in any way

artistically comparable with *After the funeral* is a subjective piece *Twenty-four years*.

Thomas has many times been stimulated to composition by the occasion of his birthday (and, for him, other people's ages seem important, too. For example, we are told that "sculptured Ann is seventy years of stone" and that "Among those Killed in the Dawn Raid was a Man Aged a Hundred".)

At the age of twenty-four, Thomas recalls his own birth: how he "crouched like a tailor" "In the groin of the natural doorway",

> Sewing a shroud for a journey
> By the light of the meat-eating sun.

The devouring powers of time are suggested with splendid condensation by the image of "the meat-eating sun" (as if that heavenly body was a man-eating tiger).

Thomas has often shown his ability in transforming the colloquial into the poetic; and in the next line the vernacular 'dressed to kill' becomes the astonishing and potent "Dressed to die". The figure of the masher or dandy, from a music-hall setting, is changed to that of the young man encountering life for the first time. But the gay promenade and encounter takes place under the laws of mortality:

> the sensual strut begun,
> With my red veins full of money
> In the final direction of the elementary town
> I advance for as long as forever is.

In comparison with the pathetic-arrogant note of "Dressed to die" and "the sensual strut", the last line strikes me as a little too clever. Contrasted with the sensuous immediacy of the earlier epithets, "as long as forever is" seems pseudo-metaphysical—a piece of elaborate tautology. But this objection against the phrase concerns its expression, not its meaning, which seems to me reasonably clear. Although the poet is "Dressed to die", he will, in one sense, live for ever; since—according to Christian teaching—a soul once born continues for ever, rejoining its own body after the latter's resurrection.

I have said that *The Map of Love* is apt to give the impression of a random collection, of variety without a central theme or core. It is true, I think, that the volume lacks the cumulative force of his two previous books; and that its proportion of first-rate poems is smaller than that of the others. Two good poems out of sixteen pieces: this is not a very assuring percentage; but it is, I believe, all we can allow in strict artistic honesty to the book.

But what is important is that we should try to understand the reason for this: for the lower number of successes in the volume, and its discrepant consti-tution—its random, miscellaneous, 'occasional' air.

The answer seems comparatively simple. In *The Map of Love* Thomas has shifted his poetical perspective a number of times. With each subject he has, so to speak, tried a different range and focus. Sometimes, as in *Twenty-four years*, the perspective is a subjective one; sometimes, as in *After the funeral*, it is objective; and sometimes, as in the sex poems *If my head hurt a hair's foot* and *How shall my animal*, it is one of identi-fication with the subject of the poem.

These shifts of ground account, I think, both for the ununited nature of the volume and for the un-satisfactory achievement of the majority of the pieces in it. Thomas, in the extension of his interests, in his growing awareness of the world of others, had not yet found his poetical sea-legs, or rather—to preserve the metaphor—he had not quite realised how much one type of vessel calls for a different tension of balance to that of another sort of craft. But these fresh mysteries he had set himself to master.

Deaths and Entrances

I

THOMAS' FOURTH BOOK of verse *Deaths and Entrances*[1] appeared in 1946. Its contents, some twenty-four pieces, showed a higher percentage of good and intelligible poems than any of the poet's previous volumes. Nor was this goodness and intelligibility manifested in one kind of poem only. There was the splendid religious poem on the nature of physical and spiritual birth, *Vision and Prayer*; a lyrical narrative fantasy—something quite new in the poet's writings— *A Winter's Tale*; the two lovely paeans of reminiscence, *Poem in October* and *Fern Hill*; the quite objective portrait, *The Hunchback in the Park*; the moving and original elegy—*A Refusal to Mourn the Death, by Fire, of a Child in London*; a statement on the nature of his poetry by the poet, *In my Craft or Sullen Art*; and a number of other pieces, all oriented to a different end and taking their departure from various vantage-points. The attempt to shift the centre of perspective—to write from a variety of view-points—which was responsible for the uncertainty and unevenness of tone in *The Map of Love*—has here been successful. The poet has at last managed to slough off his solipsistic skin, and to enter with interest and enthusiasm into

---

[1] *Deaths and Entrances* includes one poem which is not reprinted in *Collected Poems* (*Paper and Sticks*), and omits two pieces which the poet added to the latter volume (*Do not go gentle into that good night* and *Once below a time*.) *Paper and Sticks* is a gay little poem, not without a touch of real shrewdness; but somehow suggests the post-prandial exercise. The change is no doubt for the better.

the existences of others. The flexibility of imagination, the greater readiness of inspiration to respond to more numerous and diverse occasions, is what singularly marks this volume.

Nor, as yet, is there any suggestion of the poet's weariness with himself—that dying to the hopes and fears of his own spirit—discernible in his last five poems. Whenever the personal force of emotion, especially as evoked by memory, has been demanded in this volume—as in *Poem in October* or *Fern Hill*—it has been accessible to the poet.

It would, I think, be quite wrong to try and view *Deaths and Entrances* in the light of some single vision. The narrow sexual preoccupation with the world, which gave a unity to *18 Poems*, has flowered and broadened out to something far less esoteric. Similarly, though the religious note is intensely present in such poems as *Vision and Prayer*, *Holy Spring*, and *There was a Saviour*, the more nagging religious pressure of *25 Poems* has been released. The idea of damnation, which was often to be found in the poet's second book, is quite absent[2] from *Deaths and Entrances*. In part, this has been replaced by a reverent and resigned scepticism, such as we find in *The Conversation of Prayer* and *This Side of Truth*. But the nescience to which the poet admits in these poems does not destroy the mystery of the world. *Omnia exeunt in mysterium* is certainly the burden of this book as a whole. Everywhere in *Deaths and Entrances* is heard the note of individual being (whose chiefest glory is its uniqueness). We hear it in

[2] Save perhaps in the poems *Holy Spring* and *Once below a time*. In the first, love is featured as "that immortal hospital" which "made one more move to soothe/The cureless counted body". In the second, the poet seems to renounce the physical and mental exploration of his youth:

Now shown and mostly bare I would lie down,
Lie down, lie down and live
As quiet as a bone.

But I think 'damnation' is too strong a word for the acceptance of disillusionment discoverable in these lines.

the tribute to a childhood in *Fern Hill*, where the farm and the landscape of the past is remembered "In the sun that is young once only"; in *A Winter's Tale*, which celebrates a legendary happening sung by minstrels "In the departed villages"; in the exact depiction of the "solitary mister" in *The Hunchback in the Park*; and in the following lines from *Among those Killed in the Dawn Raid was a Man Aged a Hundred*:

> O keep his bones away from the common cart,
> The morning is flying on the wings of his age
> And a hundred storks perch on the sun's right hand

I have therefore thought it best to take the poems individually; and will begin by considering the best.

II

The Conversation of Prayer, the first poem in the book, is remarkably complex as to meaning. This is not on account of any characteristic impediments to understanding, often present in Thomas' verse. There are no neologisms to puzzle the intelligence, no compound words to be interpreted, and the syntax and grammar are comparatively simple. The only formal difficulty which the poem offers is that of the slowly-unfolding sentence—the sentence that takes time to arrive at its full meaning. Thus the first full-stop does not come till the eighth line (the third line of the second stanza), nor are the lines short ones. But this calls merely for careful reading, especially as to points of punctuation, but provides no real bar as to meaning itself.

What is truly difficult to construe is the final conclusion of the poem. Are the prayers answered by "the answering skies"; and, if so, are they answered in some paradoxical fashion, since

the child going to bed and the man on the stairs
Who climbs to his dying love in her high room

become "the man on the stairs" who

To-night shall find no dying but alive and warm

In the fire of his care his love in the high room.
And the child not caring to whom he climbs his prayer
Shall drown in a grief as deep as his true grave,

It is hard to know how we are intended to take this 'turning of the tables' which the prayers have effected. Are we to read the healing of the man's "dying love in her high room" as a miracle, the terms of which necessitate an exchange of the man's and the child's fate? And, if so, are we to see this paradox as part of a heavenly economy, planned by God who "works in a mysterious way"? *The Conversation of Prayer* may be described as a nexus of human hopes and fears, and the supernatural response which, obliquely, provides an answer to them.

I do not think it possible to read it as an anti-religious poem (or as a poem which mocks at the purpose of prayer). However, we must not under-estimate the thought behind the question-marks in the third stanza.

Structurally, the poem is remarkable for its use of repeated words. Each stanza has five lines; and in the course of the poem three of the end-words are repeated once; but the real hypnotic effect of repetition is obtained by taking words from the body of the line in one stanza, and then repeating them as end-words in another.

The Conversation of Prayer can also be termed as a religious poem in a minor key; a poem in which faith is not silenced, but sounds, so to speak, with the soft pedal on. But there are other poems in this volume less cautious in their declaration. *Holy Spring*, in its 'pantheistic' fashion, and *There was a Saviour* both testify after their fashion.[3] But the most assertive and positive in its statement is the long poem *Vision and Prayer*.

Some, who are uneasily alive to the virtuotistic element in Thomas' work, have classed this poem with that other *tour de force* of immoderate prolongation *Ballad of the Long-legged Bait*. The arrangement of the poem on the page in the shape of diamonds and pyramids[4] (reminiscent of George Herbert's *Wings*) has lent support to their belief that the work is largely imitative or experimental.

This opinion has further been strengthened by the religious fervour of the poem which such readers derive from the Caroline poet. With this judgment I cannot agree.

As touching the printed arrangement of the poem (which describes and celebrates birth), I have been offered another explanation. Muriel Spark has pointed out to me how the varying forms of the stanzas (the extension and contraction of the first line of each part in section one) may be taken to represent the spasms of the womb attendant on delivery. The opening lines give credence to this:

> Who
> Are   you
> Who is born
> In the next room
> So loud to my own
> That I can hear the womb
> Opening   and   the   dark   run
> Over the ghost and the dropped son
> Behind the wall thin as a wren's bone?

[3] The element of faith or worship in these poems is strong but not sustained without a break. *There was a Saviour* witnesses to the power of the idea of Christ in childhood, but notices that the succouring force of this notion has declined as the poet has grown older. *Holy Spring* speaks of that season as the time of the resurrection, but observes that this may be the last occasion for the poet to proclaim it.

[4] Henry Treece writes of the second section of the poem as "laid out in the shape of a drinking-glass, perhaps the Communion-cup, or the Grail."

In the first part of the poem, the agony and suspense of the parents before birth is presented as a kind of Agony in the Garden. This is in keeping with the development in part two, where the new-born child is associated with Christ, though not exclusively identified with him. "Genesis and Apocalypse," writes Linden Huddlestone of this poem, "coexist in the ascension of man at his true moment of origin."[5] Less metaphysically, Henry Treece observes that "The poet has openly accepted God's love, and has rejoiced in his acceptance."[6] Reading the last stanza of the poem—

> I turn the corner of prayer and burn.

—we must agree with Mr. Treece; but add that his statement leaves much to be questioned. What are the implications for the poet of his acceptance of divine love (present in this poem in the image of the sun)? They are clearly not those of orthodoxy; for in the first stanza of section two Thomas tells us,

> I pray though I belong
> Not wholly to that lamenting
> Brethren for joy has moved within
> The inmost marrow of my heart bone.

The poet's prayer to the Christ-child continues; and in it he asks that the dead shall sleep on, even though "they moan/For his briared hands to hoist them/To the shrine of his world's wound". This prayer he makes

> In the name of the lost who glory in
> The swinish plains of carrion.

"Man," as T. S. Eliot remarks, "cannot bear too much reality"; and the reality of Christ's love is felt to be a judgment he cannot face.

[5] *An Approach to Dylan Thomas* (New Writing no. 35).
[6] *Dylan Thomas* (1949).

But the Christ-child in this poem is also a mortal baby; and I am not sure that in his prayer for the child the poet does not plead for a normal human life, in which the womb[7] shall "Yawn to his upcoming" as a lover. It is possible that this passage has been influenced by D. H. Lawrence's story *The Man who Died*, where Christ's spiritual rehabilitation (as distinct from his physical recovery when he was left as good as death) is obtained at the hands of "the woman of Isis".

But whatever the reservations of faith in this poem, with the last stanza the spirit changes. No longer does the poet try to evade the pursuit of divine love. He feels himself possessed by the glory of the sun (which has followed him like "the Hound of Heaven"); and the last words are those of blessing and affirmation:

> But the loud sun
> Christens down
> The sky.
> I
> Am found

Religious in a somewhat different fashion are the two poems *A Refusal to Mourn the Death, by Fire, of a Child in London* and *Ceremony After a Fire Raid*. The title of the second poem provides us with a clue to the nature and purpose of these pieces. They are poetic "Ceremonies" or rituals, acts of commemoration and worship; even if the acts of commemoration be only for almost anonymous beings, and the worship a brief respectful love paid to their departed spirits. Indeed, in the first of these poems the poet explicitly rejects the thought of assisting at some traditional obsequies:

> I shall not murder
> The mankind of her going with a grave truth

[7] The womb may as well be death, which is the fate both of the Christ-child and the mortal infant.

For the conventional moralisms of the 'obituary' mind, he substitutes a poetic leave-taking. The poem is an anti-ceremonial ceremony.

An explanation of this poem has been offered by William Empson;[8] and with his interpretation I am substantially in agreement. A summary of this little classic of modern critical exegesis can be found in the following remarks. "This poem tells us that Dylan Thomas *isn't* going to say something. I take it that the child was killed in an air-raid, and that Dylan Thomas won't say so because he is refusing to be distracted by thoughts about the war from thoughts about the child herself or about death in general. . . . The general theme is that Dylan Thomas at death, no less than the burned girl, must be absorbed into the nature from which further life may mysteriously be born."

I dissent from this critic's interpretation only in the matter of small details. For example, of the following lines—

> Tells with silence the last light breaking
> And the still hour
> Is come of the sea tumbling in harness

—he writes, "At Doomsday the sea gives up its dead; we may be meant to think of the water *tumbling* off them, and the sea might be harnessed in that it is at last controlled." My feeling, here, is that Mr. Empson has chosen the least obvious alternative, intrigued as he so often is by "the fascination of what's difficult". But "tumbling" and "harness", I believe, do not refer to the sea in its special Doomsday condition, but merely to its usual mundane state. The waves 'tumble' (fall down and break up), and they are said to be 'harnessed' in that their ascension and dissolution follows the laws of the tide.

But this is a small enough point, and one over which

<hr>

[8] The March number of *Strand*, 1947.

I shall not linger. Mr. Empson's explanation offers, both in mass and detail, an excellent suggestive guide to the poem; and all I have to add are some ancillary remarks.

As with *The Conversation of Prayer*, much of the difficulty comes from following the slow unfolding of the sentences. The skeleton division of the first sentence (which occupies thirteen lines) is given by removing intermediary lines, and seeing the direction of the main column: "Never until the mankind making . . ./Tells with silence the last light breaking. . . ./Shall I let pray the shadow of a sound . . . to mourn/The majesty and burning of the child's death."

The second and third line of stanza one are in apposition to the first line, and the use of commas would have been helpful. But their omission is conscious and intended, in that their absence strengthens the incantatory continuity of the composition.

In "The majesty and burning of the child's death" we have a device characteristic of the poet. The normal disposition of speech in this line would be, 'The majesty of the burning child's death'; but Thomas dissociates the adjective and the noun, and makes the former serve as a noun itself. This gives to the line a greater richness and solidity; as well as juxtaposing two different ideas, "majesty" and "burning", so that they take on a sort of ritual oneness.

Ceremony after a Fire Raid features the same subject-matter as *A Refusal to Mourn*: a child burned to death when incendiary bombs were dropped. The child's forgiveness is asked, and the death spoken of as if it were a kind of sacrificial rite (by which the evil of the adult world is perhaps expiated a little). In this rite, the child is both "priests and servants/Word, singers, and tongue". The child is the sacrificial victim and yet celebrates its own sacrifice.

The last section of the poem is like a hymn or

anthem after the performance of a rite; and this time
it is an anthem of fire, in which the blazing neighbour-
hood—wherein the child met its death—and the
brightening of the dawn combine their song of praise.

There are some fine passages in this poem (as
witness the one referred to above), including the
surpassingly tender image of the dead child as "Child
beyond cockcrow". But although longer than *A
Refusal to Mourn*, it has not the latter's unity.

Writing of *A Winter's Tale*—Thomas' only true
narrative poem—both Linden Huddlestone[9] and W. S.
Merwin[10] consider it in sort as a religious composition;
the former as "an allegory of sacred love", the latter
as having connection with the old Celtic rite of the
goddess of mid-winter, whose ritual was expressive
of "the re-birth of the year", of the earth and of
man.

Both the above critics agree that *A Winter's Tale* is
one of the poet's most sustained and satisfying works.
It belongs to the class of poems represented by Thomas
Hood's *The Centaur*, George Darley's *Nepenthe*, and
Shelley's *Alastor*;[11] a class we might call the atmospheric narrative. Something happens in these poems,
and the often vague actions which occur are felt to be
symbolic, but quite of what it is hard to say. From
this, we see that this type of poem differs from
allegory, in which specific characters and actions stand
for particular persons and events.

Compared, however, with these earlier poems, *A
Winter's Tale* is simple and elementary as to the course
of the notions it expresses. There are none of those

---

[9] *An Approach to Dylan Thomas* (*New Writing* no. 35).

[10] *The Religious Poet* (*Adam* no. 238, 1953).

[11] Shelley's poem is more explicit, more didactic, than those of Hood and
Darley; but our impression of this being so is partly dependent upon
Shelley's prose preface (in which he says that "*Alastor* may be considered
as allegorical of one of the most interesting situations of the human mind").
In prose, Shelley's mind is so logical and lucid that we are easily persuaded
to accept its statements, particularly as to his own poetry.

stray unresolved conflicts, half-hidden and half-
presented by Darley in the cantos of *Nepenthe*.
Psychologically, *A Winter's Tale* might be described
as a normal wish-fulfilment fantasy in verse, a poetic
day-dream about the absence and consummation of
love. Where the likeness between Thomas' poem and
those of Shelley, Hood, and Darley lies, is in the
luxuriant sensuous description of the setting of the
tale. More than the characters (vaguely drawn figures,
in each case), the environment is made to embody and
evoke, directly or obliquely, the feelings of the hero.
The attraction of such a type of poem for a 'pantheistic'
temperament may readily be understood.

Imaginatively, *A Winter's Tale* is easy to follow; but
we may, if we choose, bear the *dénouement* of Shakespeare's play of that name in mind: from lack of love
to love discovered, both works deal with the same
transition of heart. In both works, too, there is an
element of the miraculous: in Shakespeare's play,
King Leontes encounters a beautiful statue whose
appearance infatuates him, only to find that this statue
is his beloved and living wife whom he believed to be
dead; in Thomas' poem, the loveless hero is granted
the fulfilment of his wishes through the marvellous
agency of a "she bird" "rayed like a burning bride", a
bird "woman breasted and heaven headed".

For the sake of approximate definition, we can speak,
very freely, of Thomas' poem as a 'folk-lore' variation
on Shakespeare's Renaissance setting.

One of the characteristics of this poem is the combination of simplicity of feeling (such, indeed, as
might make up a typical adolescent fantasy) with a
subtle and complex use of speech. Not that the
language of the poem presents much difficulty. The
style is not that 'gnostic' style employed in much of
25 Poems. It is lyric-narrative in tone and in purpose;
and in its fluent undulating verse, with its rhymed and

five-lined stanzas, it belongs to the group of Thomas'
best 'open' utterances which include *Fern Hill* and
Poem in October.[12] No, the quality of the language in
question does not depend on contortions of grammar,
but on the radiating and ramifying effect of its figures-
of-speech.

The poem opens with what must surely be one of the
most evocative descriptions of winter in the English
tongue. It is all as simple as a Christmas-card, the items
depicted in the first two stanzas; and yet, unlike the
Christmas-card, there is not one conventional image
present.

All the expected appurtenances of pictorialised
winter are in these stanzas: the farm in the valley, the
falling snow, and the smoke from the farm-house
chimney. But out of these old shapes has come forth
newness. The "tale" is not 'rumoured' or 'whispered'
or 'conveyed', but "ferried" by "the snow blind
twilight" over the lakes. In the descent of snow the
fields, like the flakes, are themselves described as
"floating". The steaming breath of cattle in the icy
air is exhaled "at the stealthy sail", and the valley air is
"Flocked" "with sheep white smoke of the farmhouse
cowl".

In the third stanza the figure of a man is introduced,
and in the sixth stanza he comes into closer focus:

> He knelt, he wept, he prayed,
> By the spit and the black pot in the log bright light
> And the cup and the cut bread in the dancing shade,
> In the muffled house, in the quick of night,
> At the point of love, forsaken and afraid.

Much of the appeal of this stanza, I think, resides in
the unspoken contrast between the domestic scene,
with its familiar objects, and the absence of a subject
for domestic affection.

[12] Both regular in stanza-construction, but in any strict sense unrhymed.

I have spoken of the radiating power of Thomas'
imagery in this poem, and the second and third lines
in the stanza above help to illustrate one aspect of it:
all the security, comfort, and nourishment of the
hearth is redolent in them. In their intense and primitive simplicity, they evoke early family gods—the
lares and *penates* of the Roman home. Perhaps I can
advance my meaning a little by quoting a remark by
Jean Cocteau. "A Holy Family," he once wrote, "is
not necessarily a holy family; it may also consist of a
pipe, a pint of beer, a pack of cards and a pouch of
tobacco."[13] Cocteau was talking about the grouping
of objects in a still-life canvas—an arrangement that
somehow might seem as significant as a picture of the
Holy Family. His words, however, apply equally well
to "the spit and the black pot in the log bright light",
"the cup and the cut bread" in the fire-flickering
shadows. More than standing as a cluster of images
perfectly attuned to each other, they symbolise the
deep notion of home as a place of fire, food, and shelter.
Elsewhere, Cocteau observes that behind all great
works of art are the soup-toureen and the lamp. He
means that they refer back to the stabilities of existence
—to the home, without which society and culture would
not exist.

We notice how, in the last-quoted stanza, the proverbial "dead of night" has become "the quick of night".
The play upon the term is not merely gymnastic. The
transformed phrase serves to communicate the sharp-
ness of the man's grief (as does "the point of love"),
and also the imminence of the hour. The phrase "the
point of love" suggests menace (he prays, as it were,
at the point of a sword), as well as the hidden propin-
quity of affection.

In the next stanza, the seething of desire and the
motion of prayer in the man's mind are contrasted with

[13] *A Call to Order translated by Rollo H. Myers* (1926).

the landscape's white immobility. The outside world is so still and cold that the "stables" with their horses seem changed to "statues". And as he prays, the snow becomes the snows of his childhood, "the white/In-human cradle" in which he played and lost himself; and then this image of the snow with its "always desiring centre" becomes, in turn, identified with "the bride bed forever sought". The entire landscape is charged with erotic significance:

> Deliver him, he cried,
> By losing him all in love, and cast his need
> Alone and naked in the engulfing bride,
> Never to flourish in the fields of the white seed
> Or flower under the time dying flesh astride.

And with the implication of the whole local world in his "need", death, too, becomes implicated in the beautiful image of mortality—"the time dying flesh astride".

The next two stanzas remind us that the tale to which we are attending, the tale being told with such intensity, concerns a happening long ago over:

> Listen. The minstrels sing
> In the departed villages. The nightingale,
> Dust in the buried wood, flies on the grains of her wings
> And spells on the winds of the dead his winter's tale.

Thus, the villages in which the minstrels sing, recounting this story, are no longer there. It is not "the deserted village" of Goldsmith which we are given in this poem. Here, the villages are "departed". Likewise the nightingale, which was singing when the man in this tale was alive, is dead and "Dust in the buried wood": layer upon layer of time lie atop of each other in this poem, in a way that reminds me of its treatment in the story of *Kilhwch and Olwen* in the great collection of Welsh tales, the *Mabinogion*.[14]

Twice we are commanded to "Listen" and "Look"; and the miracle at length becomes incarnate in the shape of

> A she bird dawned, and her breast with snow and scarlet downed.

This bird, who mythically represents the bride, may have been suggested to Thomas by the he-bird who mourns for his mate in Whitman's great poem *Out of the cradle endlessly rocking*. We know that Whitman was one of the poet's favourites: on the other hand, he might have taken the idea from a story out of the Celtic mythology, in which the transmigration of souls from human to animal existence is common. Again, the image of the she-bird may have presented itself quite instinctively to Thomas, the whiteness of

---

[14] I quote Matthew Arnold's *résumé* of this from his lectures *On the Study of Celtic Literature* (1867): "Search is made for Mabon, the son of Modron, who was taken when three nights old from between his mother and the wall. The seekers go first to the Ousel of Cilgwri; the Ousel had lived long enough to peck a smith's anvil down to the size of a nut, but he had never heard of Mabon. "But there is a race of animals who were formed before me, and I will be your guide to them." So the Ousel guides them to the Stag of Redynvre. The Stag has seen an oak sapling, in the wood where he lived, grow up to be an oak with a hundred branches, and then slowly decay to a withered stump, yet he had never heard of Mabon. "But I will be your guide to the place where there is an animal which was formed before I was;" and he guides them to the Owl of Cwm Cawlwyd. "When first I came hither," says the Owl", the wide valley you see was a wooden glen. And a race of men came and rooted it up. And there grew a second wood; and this wood is the third. My wings, are they not withered stumps?" Yet the Owl, in spite of his great age, had never heard of Mabon; but he offered to be guide "to where is the oldest animal in the world, and the one that has travelled most, the Eagle of Gwern Abwy." The Eagle was so old, that a rock from the top of which he pecked at the stars every evening, was now not so much as a span high. He knew nothing of Mabon; but there was a monster Salmon, into whom he once struck his claws in Llyn Llyw, who might, perhaps, tell them something of him. And at last the Salmon of Llyn Llyw told them of Mabon. "With every tide I go along the river upwards, until I come near to the walls of Gloucester, and there have I found such wrong as I never found elsewhere." And the Salmon took Arthur's messengers on his shoulders up to the wall of the prison in Gloucester, and they delivered Mabon."

its plumage suggesting the white body and attire of the bride.[15]

Next, through a landscape that recalls D. H. Lawrence's story *A Fragment of Stained Glass*, the man pursues the bird and at last attains her, "brought low" and "Burning in the bride bed of love."

Structurally, this is one of Thomas' finest poems. Psychologically, it is not his most adult. By this, I do not mean that it is immature, but that it has the same fore-shortened simplicity as the fairy tale with the happy ending. As a work of art it is perfect, as a human document just a little elementary.

Poem in October and *Fern Hill* are less religious pieces than *A Winter's Tale*. But both of these snatches of autobiography, reminiscential lyrics of the inner life, seem to be written on the assumption that "The country [of the poet's youth] is holy". Both of them are concerned with the sacrament of remembering.

The theme and development of *Poem in October* are very simple: recollection of the poet's childhood on the occasion of a birthday. Nostalgia for the past, and praise for the days that are over, are the principal feelings expressed. Looking forward to *Fern Hill* (in my estimation, Thomas' finest poem), this piece has fewer undertones of meaning, and fewer highly condensed images.

The poem does not call for minute explication. The main stages of its course are easy enough to follow: the poet rising early and setting forth, then looking back upon his town from the countryside beyond it. There, as he stands "marvelling [his] birthday away", "the weather turned round", and the landscape about him is lit with the recollected light of former summers:

The poem ends with an image of the discrepancy of

---

[15] The bird is described as "snow and scarlet downed". The "scarlet" here may have its counterpart in the idea of the bride's warm blood or possibly in her deflowering.

time: the present tense of memory, and the present
tense of the actual day and season:

> It was my thirtieth
> Year to heaven stood there then in the summer noon
> Though the town below lay leaved with October blood.

In the last lines of the final stanza, as Henry Treece
remarks, the poet seems to be "praying for another
year of life in the stability of the world he knows".[16]

> O may my heart's truth
> Still be sung
> On this high hill in a year's turning.

There may also be the idea present of aspiring to write
only—in Keats' phrase—from "the holiness of the
heart's affections and the Truth of Imagination."
"With respect to my livelihood, I will not write for it",
Keats declared in a letter to Hayden; and the finale of
Thomas' poem might be taken in much the same way,
as a prayer for integrity against the temptations of the
professional pen.

There are few obstacles in this poem to halt or
hinder the reader. Apart from a scarcity of punctuation,
and the omission of hyphens from terms that con-
ventionally call for them ("mussel pooled", "heron
priested", and "net webbed") all is comparatively
simple sailing.[17]

I have found only one teasing piece of syntax in this
poem: "the morning beckon" of line five in stanza one:

---

[16] *Dylan Thomas* (1949).

[17] In his book on Dylan Thomas, Henry Treece remarks, "What is most
interesting is that the poet, in this poem [*Into her Lying Down Head*] seems to
have abandoned his hyphenated compound words. . . . This new departure
may, consciously or otherwise, have been due to my calling his attention to
his elaborate compound words about 1938." Whereas Hardiman Scott
wrote (in *Outposts* no. 7, 1947) of *Poem in October*, "why [Thomas] doesn't
make the sensible compromise of using a hyphen when his telling epithets
like "heron priested shore" and "net webbed wall", clearly call for it, I
just can't imagine."

It was my thirtieth year to heaven
Woke to my hearing from harbour and neighbour wood
And the mussel pooled and heron
Priested shore
The morning beckon
With water praying and call of seagull and rook
And the knock of sailing boats on the net webbed wall
Myself to set foot
That second
In the still sleeping town and set forth.

At first, one expects to find a stop at "shore"; but no stop is present; and as this is the only mark of punctuation accorded its right in the poem, we must not presuppose it to be understood. The reading of the stanza falls into place, if we see it planned as a catalogue of various sensations: sound, sight, and touch ("the knock of sailing boats on the net webbed wall"). If we place the words "When" or "And I saw" in front of "The morning beckon", both sense and grammar become clear. The omission of the adverb and verb, besides being dictated by the space-pattern of the stanza, gives also an impression of simultaneity; so that what happens in the first four lines is taken to be happening, at the same time as what happens in the last five lines.

The first, and the last three, lines of the stanza demonstrate the kind of rhetoric which the poet has chosen to employ for the occasion. "It was my thirtieth year to heaven" may seem a circuitous way of stating that it is the poet's thirtieth birthday, but this 'larger-than-life-size' language corresponds to a certain amplified feeling about the event. Of the first line, Henry Treece has observed that it indicates "not only the passage of time, but the goal of his movement through time."[18] But as Thomas is, in some sense, a 'pantheistic' poet, his heaven is here and now as well as

[18] *Dylan Thomas* (1949).

beyond the grave.[19] And in this connection, I would like to quote Traherne, who writes that "Your Enjoyment of the World is never right, till every morning you awake in Heaven; see yourself in your Father's Palace; and look upon the Skies, the Earth, and the Air as Celestial Joys; having such a Reverend Esteem of all, as if you were among the Angels."[20] These are the words of a Christian 'pantheist', poetically if not doctrinally; and demonstrate how these two currents of vision can, at times, run together. Certainly, the 'pantheism' of *Deaths and Entrances* is more easily reconciled with certain Christian trends of thought, than that of Thomas' first three books.

The magnifying rhetoric which Thomas uses in his poem is seen also in the last three lines of the first stanza, where "set foot" and "set forth" almost, but not quite, embody the same idea. This device, which lends the poem emphasis, is justified also by the greater definiteness of the second verb. Together, they are like notes in a fanfare, the second more sustained and conclusive.

Henry Treece has criticised the poet for his "lack of attention to epithet",[21] and with the application of this remark to much of Thomas' work (especially in *25 Poems* and *The Map of Love*) I am in agreement; but when he instances the line "And down the other air and the blue altered sky" as furnishing examples of this, I cannot bear with him. "The other air" appears to me a poignant manner of describing the atmosphere of yester-year, the air of memory and childhood. By distinguishing between the landscape in appearance and in remembrance, the pathos of present time—

---

[19] See, for example, the poem *When I woke*, in which the poet expresses himself as identical, or co-present, with the deity:

> Every morning I make
> God in bed, good and bad.

[20] *Felicities of Thomas Traherne* ed. Sir Arthur Quiller-Couch (1934).
[21] *Dylan Thomas* (1949).

which opens like a flaw in the poet's day—is vividly
suggested. Similarly, "the blue altered sky" of the
recollecting poet—so different from "the pale rain"
which is actually falling "over the dwindling harbour"
of the town—stands justified within its context.

But if, as in these passages, Thomas uses simple
epithets, there is also to be found more complex
imagery. In the second line of the second stanza, the
poet speaks of "the birds of the winged trees flying
my name". The unusual employment of the verb here
may suggest that the pattern of the bird's flight is like
that of a sky-writing aeroplane; or if we take the verb
as transitive, then the poet's "name", which the bird
"flies", is like a banner or pennant. Both interpretations
serve to suggest a gala-occasion (that of the poet's
birthday). In the same line, too, we notice how Thomas
has detached the attribute of wings from birds and
given it to "trees", so that the tree full of birds becomes
a new sort of winged creation.

In the same stanza, there is the splendid image of the
poet's memories, pattering to right and to left about
him, as he "walked abroad in a shower of all my days".
The originality of this figure is all the more adapted
to its context, in that it has been prepared for by the
natural weather image of "rainy autumn" in the
previous line.

The poem abounds in fluctuations, corresponding
to the insecure entertainment of memories which the
poet is enjoying: "but the weather turned around"
occurs twice, and there are other references to turning;
so that the momentary peace of memory, which comes
to the poet in his nostalgia, is like the brief pause of a
veering weather-cock.

As in the poem *Fern Hill*, to which in style and
spirit this piece looks forward, there comes what a
friend of mine has spoken of as "the chill wind of fate"
—a sudden mortal sense of mutability, which Housman

expresses in his poem "Into my heart an air that kills". The entry of this intimidating current, I would locate in lines five to seven of the sixth stanza:

> Where a boy
> In the listening
> Summertime of the dead whispered the truth of his joy

The memories which, in preceding stanzas, have seemed so living to the poet, he now recognises as belonging to the dead; and, thus, as hopelessly separated from him. And yet, as in de la Mare's poem *The Traveller*, these memories are aware of him: they are watching and listening to him like a host of phantoms, so that the summer day becomes cold and haunted with them.

Thomas' chief other reminiscential piece, *Fern Hill*, has claims to be considered his finest composition. Its status is that of major poetry.

If one sought to describe this poem within the compass of a single phrase, it might be called 'an elegy in praise of lost youth'. Lament and celebration sound throughout the work: the latter strongly at the beginning, the former gaining tone as the poem progresses.

But, as with all great threnodies in English—with Milton's *Lycidas*, Gray's *Elegy*, Shelley's *Adonais*, and Arnold's *Thyrsis*—the particularity of the cause of grief is lost in a sorrow which speaks for all men. Nostalgic recollection of a child's farm holiday is the leaping-off point for the poem; but—once launched— so intense and poignant a memory overtakes the poet, that his words convey more than a merely topographical homesickness. The farm becomes Eden before the Fall, and time the angel with a flaming sword.

But no such intrusive personification operates within the poem. The farm is invested with a light as radiant as the unforfeited Garden, and time exercises its function as irrevocably as God's excluding angel. So, though at the end we are faced with nothing worse than a farm-stead which cannot be re-visited, in actual poetic terms we have experienced the states of innocence and eternity, and been subjected to corruption, time, and change.

The poem is constructed from six nine-line stanzas, with only an infrequent rhyme. The absence of rhyme suffices to make the lyrically undulating lines more natural. The artifice and architectonic of the poem consist not in the usual technical devices, but in the repetition, in later stanzas, of *motifs* established in the first. These *motifs* are not worked out with any mechanical regularity; and their place and precedence in the poem are not formally observed. The *motifs* I find to be mainly three: that of the unwitting situation of childhood; that of the delight in this situation; that of time's operation, by which the situation becomes a fate.

The first of the three is associated with such phrases as "Now as I was young and easy", "And as I was green and carefree". The second *motif* is present in "honoured among wagons I was prince of the apple towns", "green and golden I was huntsman and herdsman", "honoured among foxes and pheasants by the gay house". The third *motif* is repeated, after its initial appearance—

> Time let me hail and climb
> Golden in the heyday of his eyes

in

> In the sun that is young once only,
> Time let me play and be
> Golden in the mercy of his means,

in

> And nothing I cared, at my sky blue trades, that time allows
> In all his tuneful turning so few and such morning songs

and

> Nothing I cared, in the lamb white days, that time would
>   take me
> Up to the swallow thronged loft by the shadow of my hand,

All three motives come together in the last three lines of the poem:

> Oh as I was young and easy in the mercy of his means,
>   Time held me green and dying
>   Though I sang in my chains like the sea.

They form, as it were, a great resolving chord.

These are but three of the poem's many notes of development. In its six stanzas, we are escorted on a journey from innocence to experience. This direction also marks a journey from grace to corruption, from unity to dissolution. One of the most subtle features of this poem is the manner in which the growing presence of these latter qualities is expressed by a chilling of imagery. The first two stanzas are full of effects of sunlight; and then, in the third, nocturnal objects enter. We hear "the owls" "All the moon long" "bearing the farm away". So far, the images are not sinister; but the first touch of coolness has been conveyed.

In the sixth stanza, this chillness grows rapidly. Time takes the child

> Up to the swallow thronged loft by the shadow of [his] hand
>   In the moon that is always rising,

The eeriness of the first line, with its suggestion of an evil presence or a mysterious double in the flickering movement of the shadows, and of the ghostly appearance of the swallows in the dim lights of the loft, distils a feeling of sin and death. And now "the sun born over and over" (which assured us in the fifth stanza) yields to "the moon which is always rising"

—a symbol of the growing cold: that of a contracting imagination and heart. By the light of this moon the happy day-time vision of the farm vanished, and when the light returns it is to discover

the farm forever fled from the childless land.

Very possibly reminiscential, but in an entirely objective fashion is the poem *The Hunchback in the Park*. Thomas as a boy may be present in this piece, but all the attention is focused on the figure of the hunchback whom the boys tormented.

This poem is one of the poet's most accomplished compositions. There is no verbal turgidity within it, and no real obscurity of language. At the same time, there are examples of that compressed manner of speech—so characteristic of Thomas—as to force us to read the poem alertly.

Secondly, as to the degree of detachment—the temperamental distance between poet and subject—all is again satisfactory. The theme releases the poet from the pressure of his personal preoccupations (the sexual unrest and physiological contemplation informing so much of his poetry). But the tale or portrait of the tramp in the park permits of certain identifications with the poet. Like the latter, he is lonely: what better description could be given of Thomas' place in literature than the words he applies to the hunchback vagrant—"A solitary mister"? Then, too, in his poverty and dispossession, the tramp, like the poet, is obsessed with sex, and in his imagination

Made all day until bell time
A woman figure without fault

But in the 'setting' of the poem there are further associations with the poet. I entified, in part, with the figure of the tramp, he is also associated with "the wild boys innocent as strawberries" who, in the course of their games, make "the tigers jump out of their eyes", and persecute the tramp by calling after him and imitating his hunchback figure. Compassion for the tramp, whom the children torment, merges into nostalgia for the days when the poet himself was one of "The truant boys from the town". It is this double identification which gives the poem balance, solidity, and feeling.

Excellently contrasted, too, is the guy-like passivity of the tramp "Propped between trees and water" (one thinks of T. S. Eliot's helpless *Hollow Men*), his furtiveness and secretiveness, his sleeping at night "in a dog kennel", and "Dodging the park keeper/With his stick"; and the noisy collective aggressiveness of the boys, with their violent abrupt movements and their animal high-spirits.

The poem represents an effective fusion of the most natural daily sights and sounds (the chained fountain-cup by the boys "filled with gravel", "the fountain basin" where the poet once sailed his ship, the tramp "Eating bread from a newspaper", and the park-keeper "With his stick"), and other things, no less mundane and natural, expressed however in terms of a conceit ("the wild boys innocent as strawberries", the tramp spoken of as "the old dog sleeper"—because he slept in a lair or hovel hardly bigger than a dog's kennel, and because he is something of a lecherous old rascal; and his way of sitting down, which is compared to the water in the lake: like the water, the tramp is seden-tary. He quickly assumes a horizontal or seated po-sition. He does not stand up to things; but flees or falls flat—as the water—before them).

The poem has seven stanzas of six lines each. They are loosely rhymed, with rhymes that do not suggest contrivance. The rhythm is both natural and extremely subtle. Let us consider stanza three. The first two lines run to the same tempo; the next line is more strongly stressed; the fourth reverts to a smoother movement; the fifth flows; and the sixth begins with a stress that fades away like the echo of running footfalls.

To whom does Thomas address his poems? *In my Craft or Sullen Art* provides an answer to this question. It is one of those poems of taut simplicity which few poets are given grace enough to write. There are twenty lines to it; and the poem is made up of one eleven- and one nine-line stanza. There are five rhymes in all, and the second stanza contains no rhymes which have not already appeared in the first.

The poem is shapely as a lyric by Walter Landor; but has greater intensity, greater warmth than have most of Landor's pieces.[22]

It is also in its unpretentious unabstract mode of writing, a manifesto of Thomas' purpose as a poet. More than Verlaine's famous *Art Poétique*, it offers us superb poetry about poetry.

One of the most interesting features of this poem is the way in which original attributes are expressed by means of a single adjective, where previously Thomas would have required an epithet of many words: "*sullen* art" (because the poet must pursue his vocation in unintrusive silence, away from people), "*singing* light" (a reference to the noise which the poet's lamp is making, as well as a suggestion that it is by the light of this lamp that the poet *sings*), "*spindrift* pages" (ephemeral, since poems are forgotten, and the books in which they are written materially decay), "*towering* dead" (literature's 'mighty dead', at the same time monumental and intimidating) are examples of this.

The poem is a declaration of sympathy, of an attitude

[22] There are a number of important exceptions; but such pieces as *Death stands above me, Is it not better, Child of a day, Ah what avails*—the equal of Thomas' poems in warmth and intensity—are slighter in build; for the most part, verse-epigrams.

of identification with sympathy in its highest form—
love. "Not for ambition or bread", nor for fashion,[23]
does Thomas write—as he tells us in this poem—but
for "the lovers [who] lie abed/With all their griefs in
their arms". But these, the poet concludes

> pay no praise or wages
> Nor heed my craft or art.

although, in stanza one, he admits that it is

> for the common wages
> Of their most secret heart.

that he writes. What quite, then, is the meaning of the
poem?

The poet, I think, is saying that he wishes to celebrate the nature of love, and to represent truly the life
of the lovers' "most secret heart". He does not expect
their conscious appraisal, but perhaps he will obtain
their unconscious recognition (this seems to me the
interpretation of "common wages": it is not a
deliberated appreciation which he wishes the lovers to
give his work).

III

With one exception, the poems examined above
constitute the good and successful work to be found
in *Deaths and Entrances*. The others appear to be
flawed through obscurity, confusion, or straining for
effect. Before saying a few words upon them, I should
like to remark on the exception, a poem which Thomas
wrote for his father in his old age, *Do not go gentle into
that good night*.

Completely formal in structure, this villanelle is

---

23 " The strut and trade of charms/On the ivory stages" refers to the poets'
self-display on the printed page; and is to be contrasted with the "spindrift
pages" in stanza two. In the latter phrase the poet shows his recognition of
the limits of what he writes, and the limits, too, of its manner of appearance.

very different to the poet's earlier composition in that form, *Request to Leda*[24] which the poet omitted from his *Collected Poems*.

For all its charm, the villanelle has not been responsible for strong or forceful poems (one thinks of the artificial elegance and pathos of many of the poets of the 'Eighties and 'Nineties who cultivated this form— Andrew Lang, Austin Dobson, Edmond Gosse, Oscar Wilde, and others). But Thomas' poem is altogether forceful: it has much of the concentrated fury of expression which the poetry of the older Yeats contained, but reveals more tenderness and sympathy.

The upshot of the poem is not that the aging man should deny or reject life to the end (Thomas' father, when young, was a vociferous atheist), but that he should continue to assert his own being in the way in which he had always done. It is an exhortation to end with a bang instead of a whimper. But in asking his father to "burn and rage", the poet is only asking him not to lose heart. "Curse, bless, me now, with your fierce tears I pray", he urges. The poem is a plea for the persistence of individuality to the end, without remission.

[24] This poem was sub-titled *Homage to William Empson*, but I think it likely that there are elements of parody and satire in the piece. "Desire is phosphorus" might well refer to Empson's tendency, both in verse and prose, to convert living entities and sensuous perceptions into abstract or scientific constituents. This is so much the obverse of Thomas' fashion of thinking and writing that he may have found it a point for polite literary ridicule.

Similarly, the line "The worm is (pin-point) rational in the fruit" could be taken as a satirical comment on Empson's exacting word-for-word exegesis. The brackets, too, are in the manner of Empson's poetry and prose; and the idea that "the worm" (phallic symbol, and perhaps therefore representative of the life-force, in existence, and inspiration, in art) "is rational", or that Empsom expects it to be, might be taken as a depreciatory remark (not entirely fair) on the critic's attitude to the speech of poetry.

It is only just to mention, whether the poem is a satire or not, that Mr. Empson took it all in good part. It was published in *Horizon* in 1942; and in 1947 the critic published his excellent and laudatory appreciation of Thomas' poem *A Refusal to Mourn the Death, by Fire, of a Child in London* in the March number of the *Strand*.

There is a strong attitude of what we can call 'gay pessimism' in the poem (Yeats described the poet as one who knows that "Hamlet and Lear are gay").

The poem contains one pun ("Grave men, near death, who see with blinding sight"), and a more subtle play upon words ("Do not go gentle into that good night", where the last word suggests both the conventional expression on parting and the 'pantheistic' womb of nature to which the aging man is returning). In the line, as it stands, the epithet carries both a negative and a positive connotation. The poet begs his father not to move towards his death in a pious conventional frame of mind, but at the same time assures him that the night of existence after death will be good (since, to the 'pantheistic' thinker, nature is always good, and to be re-united to the earth through death can only be a natural and desirable resolution).

I hope these few words have helped to indicate how subtle in statement this poem really is. Read on the surface, it might be taken as the words of one atheist exhorting another, but is far from being so forthright a matter. I have spoken of the 'gay pessimism' of the poem, but recognise in my term only an approximate definition of a very complex attitude. Here, I think it sufficient to add that by 'pessimism' in this context, I am speaking of man's sense of limitation in face of his fate, and not of a belief that the world and all things in it are wryly planned.

Do not go gentle into that good night is a 'straight poem', and for that reason alone I did not treat of it in the previous section when dealing with the best work in *Deaths and Entrances*. Far from being 'straight', the other pieces I shall touch on here are 'convoluted' to a high degree, none more so that the *Ballad of the Long-legged Bait*.

Henry Treece fairly describes this composition as "54 verses, in a rough ballad form, telling what befell

when a fisherman used a beautiful young girl as bait."[25]
"Its length," continues Henry Treece, "is tiresome; it
comes more and more to lack urgency as it progresses,
and it seems at the end little more than a technical
exercise."[26]

Then, too, I find in this poem the only unfortunate
use of sex in all of Thomas' verse. The idea of the
girl hauled through the sea, affixed to the stern of the
boat, and violated by whales and fishes, seems to me an
unjustifiable theme. Unlike the story of Leda and the
Swan or Europa and the Bull, the *Long-legged Bait*
cannot plead (as far as I know) a mythological purpose.
It is true that the girl is seen, later in the poem, as
"Time" who "is bearing another son", but this is only
a random transformation. There is no developed
legendary meaning in the poem that I can discover.

Deriving almost certainly from Rimbaud's *Bateau
Ivre*, the *Ballad of the Long-legged Bait* appears to me
inferior to such minor, but interesting, poems of
imaginary voyage as *The Boat Returns* by Henry Treece,
or *After Sunset* by Vernon Watkins. Its fault, apart
from its repetitiousness, and the ill-planned manage-
ment of its narrative, lies in the over-conscious use of
Freudian symbols. Considering the themes the poet
has chosen, it is perhaps a wonder that we have not
had more of this.

There are other sexual poems in *Deaths and Entrances*,
none perhaps entirely satisfactory, yet none revealing
that crude sort of trespass which we find in *The Long-
legged Bait*. The one that steers closest to this is the poem
Into her Lying Down Head, which celebrates what the

[25] *Dylan Thomas* (1949).
[26] For a favourable verdict on the poem, see *An Approach to Dylan Thomas*
(*Penguin New Writing* no. 35). In it, Linden Huddlestone writes: "This poem
more than any other of Thomas' comes in the category of what Herbert
Read called 'absolute poetry'. It is the spontaneous welling up of an intensely personal vision, a vision that is truly apocalyptic and which over-
loads the very words trying to convey it; and yet it irresistably carries the
reader on into unfamiliar regions."

song-writers nicely refer to as "one night of love". To me, its resemblance would seem to be Lawrence's poem about the mating of whales.

> Last night in a raping wave
> Whales unreined from the green grave
> In fountains of origin gave up their love

writes Thomas, in a style of euphemism which undoes its own good work.

Into her Lying Down Head contains the striking, though repulsive, image of the shadows on the walls of the lovers' bed-room which are like "baskets of snakes"; but, for the most part, the imagery does not seem to cohere.

A finer poem with a sexual basis to it is *On the Marriage of a Virgin*. In it, Thomas contrasts the state of virginity with the state of marriage. The time chosen for this comparison is the moment of waking.

The first stanza describes a virgin's waking; and it is in keeping with the poet's sexual vision of the world that the solitary waking condition is presented in terms as erotic as is that of the married woman. For Thomas, not only human creation but all the variety of nature, whether animate or inanimate, has a body and sexual attributes. It is part of his 'pantheistic' perspective.

Thus, in the first stanza, "this day's sun leapt up the sky out of her thighs" in the same way as a child is delivered; and the morning light, like a lover, looks down upon her in the hope of finding "His golden yesterday asleep upon the iris". Neither is her virginity spoken of as a state of singleness. Her bed is referred to as the place where she "married alone", since in Thomas' work there is no single existence. All things are nubile and enter into contact.

So the poet writes of her virginity as "miraculous" and as "old" as "loaves and fishes", because—by Christ's miracle—these single objects were multiplied.

Even before her marriage, through the power of imagination (which is itself a sort of miracle) the virgin was procreative.

The second stanza, descriptive of nuptual waking, contains two excellent images which parallel those of stanza one; and serve to develop the likeness rather than the difference, of single and married life.

The seventh line of the first stanza, in a somewhat clumsy fashion, relates the love of Christ and venereal love ("doves" are proverbially the birds of Venus): "the shipyards of Galilee's footprints hide a navy of doves."

On a Wedding Anniversary provides a contrast to the above. It is a remarkably flat poem for Thomas; with a flatness which is not that of banality, but belongs rather to that order of sober deliberated statement which certain contemporary poets, particularly Robert Graves, practise. The language is original but not uplifted, and there is none of that buoyancy of rhythm which we associate with the poet.

Two other poems with erotic interest are *Love in the Asylum* and *Unluckily for a Death*. The first of these—a tender and humorous piece—is rather out of the Freudian-Romantic tradition in which the later Thomas writes about love.

Love poems tend to emphasise the common quality of lover and loved one; but Thomas, there, accents the girl's 'otherness': she is "A stranger" who has taken possession of his house.

The piece contains two characteristic plays upon common phrases: 'bolting the door at night' becomes "Bolting the night of the door", and 'at long last' becomes "at long and dear last" (by which the poet says that the girl is the last one, after many adventures, who will be dear to him).

But the conclusion of the poem is purely romantic.

Through her, the poet feels that, "without fail", he may

> Suffer the first vision that set fire to the stars.

And "the first vision" is, of course, love—which he sees as the activating cosmic force in all things, even as Dante saw it as the power

> That moves the sun in Heaven and all the stars.[27]

In *Unluckily for a Death* I can find no unity of style or meaning. The image-groups are drawn from such disparate levels ("pyre"—"phoenix", "saint"—"cloister", "she-mules"—"minatours"—"duck-billed-platypus", etc.) that I can discover no pervading atmosphere or properly circumscribing air. And of such lines as

> I see the tigron in tears
> In the androgynous dark,

I agree with Henry Treece that "one is perhaps even too humorously struck"[28] by them.

What is important about this poem, as I see it, are three detachable statements about the nature of love, which enable us to understand the poet's thought the better. The first of these posits the physical nature of love:

> All love but for the full assemblage in flower
> Of the living flesh is monstrous or immortal,
> And the grave its daughters.

Love that does not reveal itself in the act of physical consummation is, the poet feels, suspect or exceptional. It is either "monstrous" (unnatural or perverted) or

[27] Cary's translation.
[28] *Dylan Thomas* (1949).

"immortal" (sublimated); and there is also the idea that such love can have no inheritance or future. Because it cannot multiply by generation, as a physical love can do, for "its daughters" there is only "the grave".

The second statement locates the poet as responding to the 'natural' condition of love, and explains that only by the natural can the spiritual be reached:

> Love, my fate got luckily,
> Teaches with no telling
> That the phoenix' bid for heaven and the desire after
> Death in the carved nunnery
> Both shall fail if I bow not to your blessing
> Nor walk in the cool of your mortal garden
> With immortality at my side like Christ the sky.

Only by accepting the natural can we come to transcend it, and enter upon a supernatural existence. But there is also the notion, in the last two lines, of bodily and spiritual living being coterminous, the pre-requisite for which is the physical.

The last statement should be read in conjunction with the last statement of the previous poem:

> O my true love, hold me.
> In your every inch and glance is the globe of genesis spun,
> And the living earth your sons.

This Side of Truth was written for the poet's son Llewelyn, at the age of six. Henry Treece describes it as possessing "a simple human dignity, which Dylan Thomas had never before fully mastered."[29] "There is," he adds, "moreover, an admission that youth, the youth which the poet spent so prodigally in his verses, is blind, one might say false, to the truth."[29]

The poem is constructed in three formal stanzas: the first hints at predestination; the second suggests that

[29] *Dylan Thomas* (1949).

good and bad actions, like ourselves, are ephemeral; and the third that all our virtue and evil ends in the "unjudging love" of the earth, to which we return. By the word "love" more is implied here than a materialistic conception of nature. It is, in some degree, a 'pantheistic' conclusion.

To Others than You is one of the poet's few satirical pieces. It is passionate and indignant in tone, and presents us with examples of audacious speech-usage. In the first line the poet coins his own syntax:

> Friend by enemy I call you out.

Abbreviation and condensation are the determining factors here. The sense of the line, in its extended form is, obviously enough: 'Friend, by naming you my enemy, I expose you in your true colours'. By the elliptical omission of certain apprehendable words, a pungency of expression is obtained, corresponding to the poet's abruptness of temper.

The second line likewise offers us an image whose meaning appears expandable: "You with a bad coin in your socket". The cockney rhyming-word for 'pocket' contains a host of possibilities; and one of the readings of this image may be, that the false friend is a shallow or empty person, with nothing to fill the void of his nature save the thought of money. It implies also, perhaps, that the individual looks on life in terms of money; and that besides avarice there is dishonesty in his attitude (since the "coin" is a "bad" one).

There is a remarkable use of language, which I can only call a conscious mixed metaphor, in lines five to seven:

> Enticed with twinkling bits of the eye
> Till the sweet tooth of my love bit dry,
> Rasped at last, and I stumbled and sucked,

First, we are shown the friend's seductive looks and glances as something solid ("twinkling bits of eye"); this solid substance then becomes a delightful sweet, until its hollow or stony centre cause the tooth to "bite dry". From being a sweet it becomes a sort of stone, so that the poet "stumbles" on it; but, at the same time, it is not a stone on the ground, but rather a stone in the mouth. "Sucked" after "stumbled" appears incongruous, unless it suggests sucking the sore place in the mouth on which the poet's tooth "stumbled". It is, in any case, a bit of an anti-climax.

The last four lines to the poem again yield a strong and original image (the poet's friends appear as "enemies on stilts/With their heads in a cunning cloud"), but show Thomas' inability to clinch a situation with epigrammatic neatness:

> though I loved them for their faults
> As much as for their good,
> My friends were enemies on stilts
> With their heads in a cunning cloud.

"Cloud" is a poor closing rhyme to "good"; and the last two lines are Romantic in tone, while the first two are Classical. As a quatrain, it lacks unity of impact.

As another example of magniloquent diffuseness, of what one might call rhetoric out of focus, I would quote the following five lines from the poem *Deaths and Entrances*:

> On almost the incendiary eve
> Of several near deaths,
> When one at the great least of your best loved
> And always known must leave
> Lions and fires of his flying breath,

A more satisfactory use of grandiloquent language is to be found in *Holy Spring*, a not entirely successful poem.

Menace and despair, hope and praise execute an unresolved concerto. Besides this, there exist certain ambiguities of expression which do not seem justified. For example, in the second stanza—

No
Praise that the spring time is all

—there is no full-stop or comma after "No" (any more than there is after "O" in the first line of the first stanza). None the less, the sense would seem to require a pause after the negative; since without it, the general affirmative trend of the second stanza (though menace is heard in the last line) is upset.

The first four lines of the poem are the best:

O
Out of a bed of love
When that immortal hospital made one more move to soothe
The cureless counted body,

Love, as "that immortal hospital" is a peculiarly good 'contemporary' image in the strain of Baudelaire or T. S. Eliot. Another taking image, more in the poet's own line, is that of the sun "the father his quiver full of infants of pure fire".

The description of the spring-time as "all/Gabriel and radiant shrubbery" is idiosyncratic but vivid. Both Thomas and George Barker have used the name of the angel as a short-hand figure for glory and beauty; while "radiant shrubbery" serves to express the brightness and shortness of the springing green plants.

Lie Still, Sleep Becalmed is, as Henry Treece remarks, "the nearest Thomas has . . . come to the traditional sonnet".[30]

Whether the poem is a lament for one drowned at sea, or—as I incline to think—is to be taken in con-

[30] *Dylan Thomas* (1949).

junction with the next poem in the book, *Vision and Prayer*, which describes the birth of one of the poet's children, it is difficult to say. In *Vision and Prayer* the poet speaks of how he listens to "the moan/Of the mother hidden", and the "sufferer with the wound/In the throat, burning and turning" of the earlier poem makes, I believe, a like reference.

When I Woke is a kind of aubade addressed by the poet to himself. It describes the sounds of the town about him, and his reactions to these morning impressions. The poem can hardly be said to have a theme, beyond a somewhat random recitation of perceptions; and ends with the poet—displeased with the morning, drawing his sheets over his head in the pretence of being dead.

Once below a time, with its play upon the traditional fairy-tale opening, begins as something of a verbal *tour de force*, but abandons its gymnastics in the last section.

The theme of the poem is the human situation, as the poet himself has felt it, namely, that which comes from being made of "dry flesh and earth"—of being mortal.

In the first part of the poem, the poet describes his pre-natal condition:

> my pinned-around-the-spirit
> Cut-to-measure flesh bit,
> Suit for a serial sum

There is a tone of arrogance in which he speaks of his advent and childhood; but this gives place, in the last lines, to a note of resignation and humility.

The title of this poem has been attacked for its seemingly superficial perversity. But this appearance of wilfulness disappears, when we read the title and the poem in the context of Thomas' thought. "Once below a time" bears, I think, two references: one, to pre-natal existence (a characteristic preoccupation) which might be said to be *before* time (since we measure the age of a man from his birth and not from his conception); and, two, to the fact that the poem is about the poet's past life, which is irreclaimable, and may therefore be considered to be, not *within*, but *below*, time. "Below" carries with it the suggestion of 'below ground', hinting at dead or buried time, as time is in this poem.

Last Poems

I

THE FIVE POEMS that follow *Fern Hill* in Thomas' *Collected Poems*, together with the *Author's Prologue* to this volume, constitute the only separate pieces, since the appearance in 1946 of *Deaths and Entrances*, which the poet has wished to preserve.

The frequency of composition has therefore been lowered to an average of one poem per year.[1] But it would be difficult to say whether this fact signifies a diminution of poetic capacity. During this time Thomas was engaged in much other work; some purely commercial and some of literary importance. Besides lecturing in America, he produced a filmscript *The Doctor and the Devils*, a verse-and-prose play for broadcasting entitled *Under Milk Wood*, as well as further miscellaneous writings.

The six poems which remain from these years are substantial compositions, and longer than most of Thomas' pieces. What these facts seem to indicate is, that while inspiration of a worthwhile order came less seldom to the poet, its duration and strength—when it did visit him—were of considerable proportions.

The craftsmanship of all of these poems is careful: rhyme or near-rhyme are used in each case, and rhythm is handled with great subtlty. Especially is the poet conscientious over his choice of words: epithets are

---

[1] Henry Treece, analysing Thomas' rate of composition on the appearance of *The Map of Love* found it to be five a year.

quite devisedly original, and a concession to the reader is met in the occasional restoration of hyphens in the case of double-barrelled adjectives.

At the same time, a certain novelty of vision in many of the passages seems absent. There is the suggestion of a great pains-taking fabrication, often resulting in felicity of diction, but covering monotony of perception.[2] It is hard to describe the lack I feel. The artistic integrity of these poems has been so genuinely built-up that the lapse of spirit (if that is what it be) cannot easily be seen reflected in them. It is possible that some inward failing of an original force of vision can, however, be identified with the relaxed use of syntax sometimes found here. The marshalling of sentences and their clauses has never been the poet's strongest point. He has always favoured a diffuse employment of sentence-construction, and this has been one of the chiefest causes of obscurity in his work. With practice and much writing, though hardly conforming to traditional grammar, he seems in *Deaths and Entrances* to have reached a moderate mastery in these matters. I therefore feel that the following passage, taken from his poem *In country sleep* may speak of a slackening spiritual tension:

> Oh he
> Comes designed to my love to steal not her tide raking
> Wound, nor her riding high, nor her eyes, nor kindled hair,
> But her faith that each vast night and the saga of prayer
> He comes to take
> Her faith that this last night for his unsacred sake
> He comes to leave her in the lawless sun awaking
>
> Naked and forsaken to grieve he will not come.

The obscure repetitive uncomma-d run of syntax

[2] According to Coleridge, genius is the power of doing something new. If we emend this to "the power of seeing something new", I think we can apply it to the present matter, and say that, if the definition holds, the verse of Thomas since *Deaths and Entrances* manifests less of the power of genius.

from the fourth line to the end does seem to reveal some tiredness in the very process of thought.

My own conjecture is, that the poet was becoming increasingly aware of the imminence of his death. Already, in *Deaths and Entrances*, there had been oblique references to the sense of the wasting of the poet's life; and in these last poems they multiply in number and directness. In *Poem on his birthday* he writes of "The voyage to ruin I must run" and speaks of sailing "out to die". *In the white giant's thigh*—a poem about women who lie buried in a country churchyard—we have the line "Now curlew cry me down to kiss the mouths of their dust"; while two other poems, *Over Sir John's hill* and *Lament*, treat of death and the dissolution of forces.

In a sense, I think we can say that the freshness of the poet's vision was probably spent in *Deaths and Entrances*. With the publication of that book, it seems that an originality of conception, which had informed the poet's work since the days of *18 Poems*, had lost most of its power. This did not affect the originality of language in these later poems which are, if anything, perfected by greater care and labour. But between the perfecting of a medium and the development of inspiration there is a subtle difference; and this difference is what we detect in Thomas' last poems.

Another feature of this change is the greater emphasis on descriptive, as opposed to expressive, writing. This is a slender distinction to draw; but the point I wish to stress can be made by remarking that in these later poems the amount of what we ordinarily term 'descriptive poetry' is greater than what we find in his earlier work. His poems take in more of the outside world; and the cultivation of exterior surfaces, as distinguished from inner essences, increases. It is as if the poet had felt that his own particular destiny was fixed, that his spirit's journey was chiefly accomplished; and had turned to the outside world for relief from his own self-weariness.

Such an attitude makes, in part, for a Virgilian poetry; and what we get in Thomas' last poems is something blander, sweeter, and more resigned than we have had from him before. Of course, the term 'Virgilian' is to be understood here relatively. The strange exhausted fury of *Lament* is quite alien to the Roman poet. I use the word because it suffices to signify the verbal craftsmanship, an approach to language of loving care, and a limiting of subjective expression.

Not that the world we get in these poems is the world in the eyes of everyman. Nature, here, is viewed through a film of intensely personal feeling; and things are described, as it were, through a veil of tender and vivid leave-taking. "I opened the leaves of the water at a passage/Of psalms and shadows", wrote the poet,

> And read in a shell,
> Death clear as a buoy's bell.
> (*Over Sir John's hill*)

This voice, I think, he often heard speaking.

II

The first of these poems, *In country sleep*, is a tender and gentle exorcism of a child's fearful imagination. The poet addresses the little girl and assures her that the terrors she thinks to meet in dreams are not to be believed on. "The wolf in a sheepwhite hood" out of "the land of hearthstone tales" is not to be feared: the apparition has no power. The only spirit that has real right-of-way in "country sleep" is God "the

Thief",³ and he is "meek as the dew". "Meek as dew
blown to the thorn", God, he tells the child, comes
"this night" "and night without end. . . ./Since you
were born".

In the Epistle of Peter, "the day of the Lord" and
Christ's second coming is associated with judgment
and presumably with death. The poem seems also to
associate the two. The words "this night" "and night
without end" may have been prompted by the lines,

> This ae nighte, this ae nighte,
> —*Every nighte and alle*,
> Fire and sleet and candle-light;
> *And Christe receive thy soul.*

from the *Cleveland Lyke Wake Dirge*, "a watch-song
sung over dead bodies", in which the thoughts of
death, God, and judgment are closely juxtaposed.
God, in the figure of "the Thief", seems to be both
the bringer of fear or death and the gentle inspector
of our faith. But the child's faith, says the poet, shall
be proof against these fears:

> And you shall wake from country sleep, this dawn and each
>   first dawn,
> Your faith as deathless as the outcry of the ruled sun.

The whole poem is a paradox, since it partakes of
religious thought, and religious truth—as Kierkegaard

---

³ Thomas was clearly recalling the phrase "like a thief in the night"; but
whether he knew or implied its context (*The Second Epistle of Peter, Chapter
three, verse ten*) in the poem, it would be difficult to decide. I myself incline
to believe so. Verses nine and ten of the Apostle, if borne in mind, certainly
give a richer, deeper note to a reading of the poem:
  9. The Lord is not slack concerning his promise, as some men count
slackness; but is longsuffering to us-ward, not willing that any should
perish, but that all should come to repentance.
  10. But the day of the Lord will come as a thief in the night; in the which
the heavens shall pass away with a great noise, and the elements shall
melt with fervent heat, the earth also and the works that are therein shall
be burned up.

observed—is a paradox—an offence to reason. For though the poem appears to assure us that "Death shall have no dominion", there is much sadness in the work, as of one dwelling on an imminent farewell. The poet speaks, for example, of "the stern bell" which

> talks
> In the tower and tolls to sleep over the stalls
> Of the hearthstone tales my own, lost love; and the soul walks
> The waters shorn.

But the diffused poignancy informing the poem is balanced by a sense of the beauty, the venerable beauty, of the landscape. The dreamland and restland of "country sleep" are blended in the poem with the night-life of nature; and are viewed by the poet in a religious light:

> Out of a saint's cell
> The nightbird lauds through nunneries and domes of leaves
>
> Her robin breasted tree, three Marys in the rays.

"The country is holy: O bide in that country kind" —this is the central intuition of the poem; and with this intuition there goes an exhortation: to "bide in that country kind", to stay within the realms of a life as religious as it is instinctive.

One of the features about the passage quoted, and about the poem in general, is the explicit addition of ritual imagery to religious thought and emotion. It may be remarked how these images are not drawn from the tradition of one Church alone, but are selected from opposed religious traditions. "Saint's cell", "nunneries", "the rain telling its beads" derive from Catholicism, while "the lord's-table of the bowing grass", and the "black bethels" of the rooks (section two, stanza one) refer to Protestant worship. Nor is the

Christian Faith the only source from which these images are taken, for there is also the Buddhistic figure of "the prayer wheeling moon". This commingling, I think, has been employed by the poet advisedly. Not only does it introduce variety into a decorative scheme but corresponds to the poet's undenominational feeling. (I cannot believe that, for Thomas, truth could ever appear to reside in one religion solely.)

Structurally, the poem is one of the most formal and sustained of all Thomas' out-put. The first section consists of nine stanzas of seven lines each, with the rhyme-scheme ABCBAAC (three rhymes per seven lines), and the second section of eight stanzas of six lines each, with the rhyme-scheme ABBCCA. This rhyming regularity and tightness is an unusual element in Thomas' poetry, but one to which his development from *Deaths and Entrances* strongly progressed.

From an artistic stand-point, I regard *In country sleep* as an almost perfect poem. The unclarified syntax of stanza seven of section two seems to me the only flaw in an otherwise pure stream of recititive lyricism.

Over Sir John's hill continues the cultivation of rhyme which we have seen the poet pursuing. The poem has five stanzas consisting of twelve unequal lines, and to these twelve lines six rhymes are given, with the following consistent arrangement: AABCCBDEAFF. This self-allotted pattern cannot have been easy to follow, and represents a greater discipline of rhyme than the poet had ever set himself before. As it is, Thomas accomplishes his task by resorting to such near-rhymes as "shell" and "elm", "knelled" and "elmed", and by basing the last two rhymes of the stanzas upon an initial like consonant and vowel: "heron"/"headstone", "passage"/"prancing", "dingle" /"distant", etc.

In some respects, I feel, this poem may be compared

with Gerard Manley Hopkins' *Spelt from Sibyl's Leaves*. There is, in both, the too earnest cultivation of a pattern to allow for the free-play of natural expression. As art-statements, the two poems have very much to recommend them; but the best poetry offers, in the one composition, human and artistic statement together. Not that I am saying that *Over Sir John's hill* reads falsely as a human statement. It is only that its speech does not possess that high easiness of expression which belongs to the poet thoroughly at home in his chosen idiom. The poem's intricate artistic use of language has not, truly, the same unnaturalness which we find in *Spelt from Sibyl's Leaves*. Conversely, it does not manifest the confident usage of an intricate form which, say, Coventry Patmore's Odes in *To the Unknown Eros* exhibit.

For all that, *Over Sir John's hill* marks another step in Thomas' last phase: his pursuit of a poetry of craftsmanship.

The poem is a kind of elegy—for young birds killed by a hawk above the River Towy, close by the poet's home. It is closely and intricately descriptive (and it is this, together with the rhyming-scheme, which slows up the tempo of the poem, and sometimes suggests a lack of compulsion). The poem is also remarkably objective; though the theme of death and fate, as applied by the poet to the birds, seems to reverberate back upon him.

In *Poem on his birthday* Thomas returns to a more subjective exploration. It is written in twelve nine-line stanzas, and is tied to no rigid rhyming-system, though great play is made with the use of like vowels in the end-words of the stanza.

The first four stanzas are chiefly descriptive, and serve to locate the poet in a natural setting. This setting is the same as in the last poem: from his cliff-side vantage-point the poet watches the herons, and the gulls, and the hawks hunting for their prey. The death of their victims is seen as given in the scheme of things; and the idea of this fate, this death, is seized upon by the poet who, in "the ambush of his wounds", "sings towards anguish", his own appointed end.

The next four stanzas prospectively explore the dark and death into which the poet goes. They begin with a note of despair, as the poet reflects on the inextricability of his situation. From his predicament, there is no escape this side the grave:

> And to-morrow weeps in a blind cage
> Terror will rage apart

This, he knows, is the prison in which he must live,

> Before chains break to a hammer flame
> And love unbolts the dark
>
> And freely he goes lost
> In the unknown, famous light of great
> And fabulous, dear God.

The last three lines, conveying relief and a sense of unendurable pressure ended, are followed by lines of more qualified import.

> Heaven that never was
> Nor ever will be is always true

writes the poet, in a paradox even more self-contradictory than the paradox in *In country sleep*. Death is a land, the poet tells us, where "he might wander bare"

> With blessed, unborn God and his Ghost
> And every soul His priest.

But death and its freedom still lie ahead; and before the poet arrives there he must suffer the immediate future, and "dark is a long way".

In the next stanza, the despair of the poet reaches its apex, in the thought of

> The voyage to ruin I must run,

and then, as it were, suddenly turns the corner with the decision to

> Count my blessings aloud:

The last three stanzas elaborate this intention:

> the closer I move
> To death, one man through his sundered hulks,
> The louder the sun blooms
> And the tusked, ramshackling sea exults;

"As I sail out to die" writes the poet in the last line of all; and this poem may be described as Thomas' *Ship of Death*. More elaborately composed than D. H. Lawrence's poem of that title, Thomas' piece has not the same clarity of thought and strong simple rhetoric. More interesting as a work of art, and sincere without doubt as a human statement, *Poem on his birthday* has not the same strong unity of testament which makes Lawrence's poem so convincing. It says too many things to say one thing powerfully.

Like all of Thomas' last pieces, it is studded with exquisite and original epithets: "the mustardseed sun", "the livelong river", "tumbledown tongue", "ramshackling sea", and a swarm of others.

Lament, the next poem, is perhaps Thomas' most objective composition. It tells the story of a 'roaring boy'; his uprise, dissolution, and downfall. As a dramatic character-study, told in a balladic fashion, it is altogether successful. In its crude lewd manner, it is grim and pathetic; as human, humorous, and sad as Villon's *Ballad of Fat Margery*. And behind the completely sustained 'external' style of writing, we feel that here is much of the poet, a part of his own swashbuckling existence. But it is obviously only a part; and the disguise is more effectively maintained by the poem being clearly cut to a pattern—the given traditional pattern of bawd. And the poet's success is very much assisted by the amount of rich stylistic comment which Thomas is able to work into this genre. As much as Yeats' *Crazy Jane* poems or his sequence *A Woman Young and Old*, Thomas' *Lament* can be taken as offering "a criticism of life". It is not bawd for bawd's sake, nor bawd for instruction's sake either. It is experience and reflection, the which together comprise such 'criticism'.

Structurally, the poem is excellent, comprising five stanzas of twelve lines each, with six rhymes thus arranged: ABCDABCDEFEF. Each stanza has a slightly varied refrain, and two first lines more freely varied; while the last stanza substitutes an inverted A rhyme—"bells jaw—"/"bore angels"—for the second C rhyme.

Of all Thomas' poems, *Lament* may be considered the most Parnassian, both in the sense in which the French school of poets used the term and in the sense in which Hopkins used it.[4] It has that objectivity, that writing from *outside* the subject, together with the attention to regular form and close rhyming, which the French school prescribed; and it has the easy control of a familiar idiom which the Jesuit poet implied by the term.

Parnassian, certainly, is the nemesis that falls on the libertine, whose "sunday wife" bore him angels, and

[4] According to Hopkins, Parnassian poetry "is spoken *on and from the level* of a poet's mind, not, as in the other case, when inspiration, which is the gift of genius, raises him above himself. *Parnassian* then is that language which genius speaks as fitted to its exaltation, and place among other genius, but does not sing . . . Great men, poets I mean, have each their own dialect as it were of Parnassin, formed generally as they go on writing" (Letter to A. W. M. Baillie, Sept. 10, 1864). But perhaps there is more inspiration in Thomas' *Lament* than is allowed for in this general definition.

plagued him to death with "all the deadly virtues".
Parnassian, too, is the ordering of the poem with its
Aristotelian 'beginning, middle and end'. I quote the
fourth penultimate stanza, as much for its mordant
psychology, as for its brilliant expression:

> When I was the half of the man I was
> And serve me right as the preachers warn,
> (Sighed the old ram rod, dying of downfall),
> No flailing calf or cat in a flame
> Or hickory bull in milky grass
> But a black sheep with a crumpled horn,
> At last the soul from its foul mousehole
> Slunk pouting out when the limp time came;
> And I gave my soul a blind slashed eye,
> Gristle and rind, and a roarer's life,
> And shoved it into the coal black sky
> To find a woman's soul for a wife.

The idea and image of the soul's eye ("blind" and
"slashed") as the male member is especially audacious.

In the white giant's thigh, excepting only the long
Author's Prologue (in verse) to the *Collected Poems*, is
Thomas' last separate composition in verse, and constitutes a splendid conclusion for one whose chief
poetic interest has been in the life of sex. The swan-song
of a poet equally dedicate to Venus and Apollo, *In
the white giant's thigh* is a superb erotic poem. It is as
purely free from the bawdy as *Lament* is crammed with
it. It is not the joke of procreation but the memorable
lyricism of sex[5] which this poem magnificently conveys. Not that its animality is omitted. The physical, in
all its over-powering beauty, is made to obtrude, to
cry out for recognition. The pastoral loves of Daphnis
and Chloe, no longer innocent, and long since dead
and buried, speak through this poem, unappeased and
anguished. A fantasy which tells the truth concerning
man's perennial sexual hunger and woman's perennial

---

[5] As Baudelaire observed in *My heart laid bare*, "F . . ing is the lyricism of
the people".

need for children, it forms a resplendant and fitting
drop-curtain to the poet's persistent saga of sex.

The theme of the poem is 'a day-dream' by moon-
light in an ancient country graveyard. The poem
imagines the buried women calling out still for love:

> Through throats where many rivers meet, the women pray,
> Pleading in the waded bay for the seed to flow

The poet elaborates further on their pasts, bringing
the warm atmosphere of their loves once more into
focus with exact touches. And when he has evoked the
sense of physical longing in their lives, and located it
in the erotic fertile life of nature, he speaks of feeling
their compulsion upon him. "Now curlew cry me
down to kiss the mouths of the dust", he writes,
finding in the idea of death the thought of love's
rehabilitation:

> Teach me the love that is evergreen after the fall leaved
> Grave, after Belovéd on the grass gulfed cross is scrubbed
> Off by the sun

To his 'pantheistic' imagination, the dead women
are still desirous; and the poem ends with a flaring
image:

> the daughters of darkness flame like Fawkes fires still.

Each four lines in this poem follows the rhyme-
scheme ABAB, so that a new set of rhymes begins with
each fifth line. But these four-line rhymings are not
arranged in regular quatrain-form, falling into their
own verse-paragraphs according to the demands of the
poet. Every line in this poem reveals the intricate
labours of its maker. And to the intricacy of its
shaping there goes an original freshness of perception.
"The pitching clouds", "ox roasting sun", "gooseskin
winter" are a measure of this rareness.

Nor is emotion or compulsion absent. The theme commemorates the poet's past interests; and, in its equation of love and death, looks forward to the poet's future.

All it lacks is inspiration's highest working; by means of which the world is recreated anew, one step ahead of the poet's last production. The perspective and vision of this poem belong to Thomas' past achievement. Its beauty is 'Alexandrian'—a magnificent flowering of one marking time on a spot beyond which he is not to advance.

Of the *Author's Prologue* to the *Collected Poems*, John Davenport[6] has observed how Thomas once asked him if he had ever examined the poem. "If I bothered to do so, he said, I would find that it was 102 lines long, in two halves of fifty-one lines, the fifty-first line rhyming with the fifty-second, the fifty-third with the fiftieth, and so on cyclically until line 102 would be seen to rhyme with line one." The forethought and dexterity of this plan, of what D. G. Rossetti termed "fundamental brain-work", are obvious. And no less excellent is the passing care with which each line of the poem is written.

In part, we can read it as a catalogue of natural glories, of animal, marine and botanical enchantments surrounding the poet's house in Laugharne, and now explicitly recorded in praise.

"Hark", writes the poet, in two lines that recall the attitude of the *Psalms*,[7]

> Hark: I trumpet the place,
> From fish to jumping hill!

He tells us that he builds the "ark" (of his poem),

> To the best of my love
> As the flood begins.

[6] *Dylan Thomas* by John Davenport (*Twentieth Century Review*, Dec., 1953).
[7] In verse four of *Psalm 114* we read that "The mountains skipped like rams, and the little hills like lambs."

What is this flood which the poet anticipates? I think there are several connotations to it: first, perhaps, the flood of the incoming tide on the seashore close to his house; secondly, the flood of autumn and winter (the poem was written at "God speeded summer's end"); thirdly, it may be the flood of middle-age; fourthly, it may be the flood or apocalypse of history (see lines nineteen to twenty-two in the first part of the poem); and, lastly, it may be death.

In the first section of the poem, Thomas' poetry is described as a "rumpus of shapes", its purpose being to "Glory . . . this star", and the condition of writing it as being one of "poor peace".

The second part contains a loving praise of Wales, and asserts the poet's community with his

> kingdom of neighbours, finned
> Felled and quilled,

to which he is united by God's "beasthood"—a particularly 'pantheistic' expression.

The last lines of the poem read, in retrospect, like a farewell; but perhaps we are wrong to take them as such. However, I find it difficult not to associate Thomas' "ark" that "sings in the sun" and Lawrence's out-going "ship of death". Whatever may be the import of the ark-image in the *Author's Prologue*, the poem as a whole suggests fulfilment, and knowledge of a personal unique work done.

Critics, Style and Value

I

THOMAS, AS A poet, seems to me an extraordinarily difficult figure to summarise. Part of this difficulty arises, I think, from the non-intellectual nature of his work (Henry Treece[1] considers him the least intellectual poet of his generation), which cannot easily be reduced to a formula without distorting its intention or meaning. It is true that there is a consistency discoverable in his work, but it is one that derives from a certain prevailing atmosphere rather than from a number of recurrent concepts. The continuity in Thomas' work is not the continuity of rational argument, but of something like biological growth. His poems evolve by a mode of transformation rather than by a step-by-step advance.

Because of this, it would appear that the intuitive critical approach to Thomas' verse as a whole is uncalled-for. What seems required is a sympathetic word-for-word unravelling of the separate poems; and in the attention which certain of his pieces received from Francis Scarfe, William Empson, Henry Treece, and Marshall W. Stearns, fortunate precedents were established.

This is not in any way to belittle the early statements which Sir Herbert Read and Dr. Edith Sitwell made about his poems; for when the former wrote that "these poems cannot be reviewed; they can only be

Dylan Thomas (1949).

acclaimed", describing them as constituting "the most absolute poetry that has been written in our time",the purpose of the words was not to define but to draw attention to a new phenomenon. And that attention once secured (largely through the commendation of these writers), the next task for criticism was to undertake an examination of these strange poems one by one; and only then to pronounce upon the generality of Thomas' muse.

Ironically, the very school one would have expected most fitted for this business—the textual analysts[2] associated with Dr. Leavis of Downing College, Cambridge, and the magazines *Scrutiny* and *The Critic*—failed lamentably to interpret or evaluate the poet. Both these magazines which came out against the work of Thomas have since ceased publication, and were it not for one factor, the inability of their contributors to recognise the positive achievement of the poet could conveniently be forgotten. The factor that precludes such happy oblivion as the most sensible comment, is that *Scrutiny*, in particular, played an important role in forming the taste of teachers of English in many of the higher schools in this country for something between ten and fifteen years. This being so, a few short remarks on the spirit of these critics may be spared.

Writing in *Scrutiny* (Summer, 1946), Mr. Wolf Mankowitz concluded that "Mr. Thomas does not offer very much to the literary critic for analysis. He is responsible for a great deal which transcends analysis in the work of other young writers. He offers at best

[2] Although affiliated to this group, a critic of the stature of William Empson, in his excellent exposition of Thomas' poem *A Refusal to Mourn* (*Strand*, March, 1947), proved conclusively that fine natural sensibility must always transcend group prejudice and fashion. It is amusing and instructive to compare Empson's masterly exegesis of this poem with the carking "superior" bafflement which Mr. Henry Gibson proudly displays, as his only critical trophy from the poem, when he came to examine the same piece in *The Critic* (Autumn, 1947).

an appeal to the sophisticated eye on the look-out for the cheap *frisson* of recognising a trick which some other competitive poetry-lover lost." Apart from the severity of judgment and the acerbity of tone, which certain of Dr. Leavis' followers appear to have inherited from him, there is nothing in this statement which might make the reader suspicious of the critic's credentials. It has the authoritative pitch, and that—with many—passes for wisdom. But when we turn to Mr. Mankowitz's responses to the poet's actual lines and phrases, the shortcomings of his sensibility are obviously apparent.

Speaking of what he calls Thomas' "false analogies", Mr. Mankowitz remarks that "a variety of 'striking' images such as 'the children innocent as strawberries' . . . fall down as soon as analysed." That Mr. Mankowitz is unable to sense the likeness between the unreflecting rosy-cheeked children and the fresh, red, unspoiled fruit ("innocent" because uncorrupted, uncorrupted because they are not rotten), shows that his own notion of analogy is narrowly, pedantically, inadequate. The same inflexibility of mind is present when he complains of such a "poetic pseudo-statement" as the phrase "happy as the grass was green". What Thomas is referring to here is surely common knowledge to all who remember their childhood (which is the context of the poet's phrase). When one was younger the grass seemed greener; and this intenser hue of the grass is used as a measure of the poet's happiness when he speaks about his boyhood.

The critic who cannot see the justification for running counter to accepted speech-forms in such phrases as this would seem to reveal a too niggardly awareness for us to trust in his conclusions.

II

I have already indicated my hesitation in sum-
marising Thomas' poetry as a whole. For what it is
worth, one can easily talk of how his early 'body'
poetry, with its centre in subjective sensation, has
tended to evolve towards a more traditional descriptive
poetry, with its centre in the object depicted. But this—
though helping to determine the direction of the poet's
writing—presents no general image of it, and does not
suggest its over-all nature.

The difficulty of arriving at such a formulation is
especially seen when we attempt to frame a general
definition of the poet's style.

To by-pass this difficulty by maintaining, with
Geoffrey Grigson, that there is no style there at all—
only a discrete formlessness "with the meaningless
hot sprawl of mud"[3]—does not seem a particularly
felicitious solution.

One of the best attempts to locate a characteristic
method of Thomas is made by Cecil Day Lewis in his
book *The Poetic Image*. Commenting on the poet's own
account[4] of how he wrote his verse, the critic observes,

[3] In the essay *How much me now your acrobats amaze* in his book *The Harp
of Aeolius* (1947).

[4] In a letter to Henry Treece, Thomas wrote that "a poem by me needs a
host of images. I make one image—though 'make' is not the word; I let,
perhaps, an image be 'made' emotionally in me and then apply to it what
intellectual and critical forces I possess; let it breed another, let that image
contradict the first; make of the third image, bred out of the two together,
a fourth contradictory image, and let them all, within my imposed formal
limits, conflict. Each image holds within it the seed of its own destruction,
and my dialectical method, as I understand it, is a constant building up and
breaking down of the images that come out of the central seed, which is
itself destructive and constructive at the same time. . . . The life in any
poem of mine cannot move concentrically round a central image, the life
must come out of the centre; an image must be born and die in another;
and any sequence of my images must be a sequence of creations, recreations,
destructions, contradictions. . . . Out of the inevitable conflict of images—
inevitable, because of the creative, recreative, destructive and contradictory
nature of the motivating centre, the womb of war—I try to make that
momentary peace which is a poem."

that "At the centre of Mr. Thomas' poems there is not a single image, but 'a host of images'. For the reader the impression may be of an escape of gas under water—I do not intend this with any disrespect —and bubbles breaking out apparently at random all over the surface: for the poet, the bubbles are the heart of the poem. Secondly, the process by which this host of images creates a poem is one of conflict—the second image will 'contradict the first', and so on. Now, in what sense can one image be said to contradict another? Logic is obviously not in question. Nor, I think, are we chiefly concerned with that kind of physical antagonism between image and idea which produces conceit, although such conceit can sometimes be found in Mr. Thomas' verse, as for example the Crashaw-like second line of

> A hand rules pity as a hand rules heaven;
> Hands have no tears to flow.

Nor, again, is it a matter of the poet letting one image follow another into the poem automatically just as they pass through his mind, for Mr. Thomas speaks of applying 'intellectual and critical forces' to his images, and of 'imposed formal limits'. By 'contradiction' I think we must understand the bringing together, in images, of objects that have no natural affinity; or perhaps it might be more accurate to say objects which would not on the face of it seem to make for consistency of impression."[5]

This tells us much about Thomas' style, but in terms of cause rather than effect. Is there any simple way by which we can suggest the predominant quality of Thomas' finished poetic speech?

[5] For a most fruitful application of this principle of composition to Thomas' poem *After the Funeral*, the reader is referred to pp. 123–125 of Mr. Day Lewis' book.

One American critic has summed-up his impression of Thomas' verse by referring to the poet's "style of sound". This term, which implies a recognition both of the rhetorical and incantatory elements in Thomas' work, applies extremely well to the early poems, but does not characterise the high proportion of visual and factual imagery in the verse from *Deaths and Entrances* onwards. In these later poems, what Thomas appears to be striving after is not an interpretation of experience, but a sensuous verbal equivalent for it— for a body of words which should have the density, the logic-proof nature of sensation itself.

But between the style of these later poems and his early 'auditory' pieces, can there be said to be any likeness? I think there can; and find the clue given in an excellent essay on the poet by M. Roger Asselineau.[6] M. Asselineau speaks of how from the first line of a poem by Thomas, one is precipitated in *media res*. "The openings of his poems," he observes, "possess a surprising brutality: 'I see the boys of summer [in their ruin]', 'My hero bares his nerves along my wrist', 'If I were tickled by the rub of love'. Titles are never employed by him. A title is already the start of explanation, and to make any concession to the reader is something repugnant to him."

In remarking how a poem by Thomas precipitates us into the thick of the situation which it expresses, M. Asselineau leads us to consider the autotelic method of this poet's composition. By severing the ropes of intellectual relativity, which tether most poems to a set of circumstances not immediately poetic, Thomas has largely fashioned a style intended as impenetrable to the 'prose' mind. In the early poems, this resistance to reason is embodied in a style whose suasions are rhetorical and incantatory: in the latter poems, the chief device against the inroads of rational thought is a

[6] *Etudes Anglaises* (Janvier, 1954).

close-packed sensuous imagery—a sealed column of verbalised sensation.

So far, then, as Thomas' poetry repudiates all intercourse with non-poetic thought, his style may be said to reach out after a verbal ideal of glorious isolation. But this should not lead us to think of his verse as the latest bloom of 'pure poetry'; since by that epithet is often understood a poetry whose content, as well as form, is verbal—a poetry whose subject itself is words. Unlike the work of the exponents of this school, the poetry of Thomas is not *about* words. It is about memory and sensation—and all the ingredients of experience, in fact—but always about experience from within: about sensation, by one engaged in it; about memory, by one remembering. The abstracts of these states—which is what the rational reflective mind usually deals in when it comes to them—was anathema to the poet. What he wrote from was the act of experience—the condition of fashioning it or enduring it; and what he wrote with was rhetoric and imagery—the warm simulacra of experience in words.

III

To locate Thomas' position in English poetry at the present time would be premature. His death has stirred most of us to a greater degree of willing sympathy than probably makes for the justest criticism; and this is as it should be. Certainly we need, at the moment, to approach his work with the most voluntary feelings of identification possible. We need to submit ourselves to the enchantments of his verse, and shall come away with our sensibility the richer. But before we can be sure how much the richer we are for this contact, the clarification of time is necessary. To-day we stand too close to our subject: perspective is demanded, and the years will provide it. What I have to say, then, in this postscript, concerning the place and status of the poet, can only be advanced as conjectural and tentative in the extreme. In offering the substance of my critical hazard, I hope that the avoidance of two extremes will be conducive to moderation in future and more definite assessment of the poet.

In regarding the poetry of Thomas, and the interest attached to it of late years, we must allow for the working of three factors: literary fashion, literary history, and intrinsic literary merit. The first of these is of course a powerful but ephemeral force. The fashion for Thomas was doubtlessly created by the very violence of the poet's shock-tactics (quite outside a consideration of their real poetic efficacy); and such renown as Thomas owes to the agency of this force will essentially diminish with the years. But likewise, too, the counter-fashion—current among the disciples of Dr. Leavis, and the admirers of Lord Gorell—will wane, perhaps even more rapidly.

Of more durable consideration, in the assessment of Thomas, is his achievement in extending literary technique. To instance but one of the devices by which he had enriched poetic usage—his adaption of colloquialisms to a lyrical end and purpose. Already, in the 'Twenties, T. S. Eliot had caused an appreciable stir by inserting phrases from common speech, bare and unworked, into his verse. But with the alien presence of such 'prose' words, Thomas was not content. And so, in his verse, we get such figures as "a grief ago" (for 'a while ago'), "happy as the heart was long" (for happy as the day is long'), and "the man in the wind and the west moon (for 'the man in the moon and the west wind'). Certain of these poetic variations have been spoken of aversely by critics; but whether or not examples of this device in Thomas' poems can be considered successful, the fact remains that the method has added to the sum of poetic equipment.

Another aspect to be observed in Thomas' contribution to literary history is the revival which his work occasioned of a more lyrical manner of writing. The naturalisation of the poetic idiom, which the Imagists began, had—by the middle of the 'Thirties—gone so far that an unnatural flatness resulted. Instead of the varying speech-rhythms which Eliot's generation had wished to assimilate, we were offered, too often, the rhythms of prose, along with 'prose' thoughts and sentiments. From this level of melodic dullness, Thomas' work helped to awaken us; and without evaluing over-highly the neo-romantic movement which followed, we must allow a number of good poems which Thomas' verse helped to incept.

To decide what proportion of the poet's present fame derives from his intrinsic literary merit is a much harder issue. Stating the matter without too much fine point, I should say that about one-third of the poems in his *Collected Poems* (which contains ninety-nine pieces) represents good or near-successful work. The remaining two-thirds seems to me sadly marred by a variety of faults: strained and wilful mannerisms, mystifications, and needless obscurities. That it will continue to be studied for the light it throws on the better pieces, and that such study will increasingly reveal isolated triumphs of language, appears to me also certain. Yet Thomas' status will, I think, be determined by the smaller body of his poems; and the size of this body will necessarily limit his lasting renown. At the same time, we might well remember that the ages of great out-put in verse seem over, and not place too much stress on bulk as a criterion.

But neither in the number of his worth-while pieces nor in the length of his individual poems was

Thomas remarkable. One of his (by common consent) finest compositions, *Fern Hill* is some ten lines shorter than Shelley's *Ode to the West Wind* and over half as short as Gray's *Elegy in a Country Churchyard*. Of his other poems, there are not more than a dozen of equal or greater length than *Fern Hill*, and probably not one quite as good.[7]

These comparisons are not intended to provide a more than quantitative perspective; but they are not without some bearings on the status that Thomas will come to assume. If T. S. Eliot had not written *The Waste Land* nor any of the *Four Quartets*, he would be—as far as out-put is concerned—a poet of the same calibre as we have to assess in Thomas.

Among Thomas' shorter pieces are some half a dozen which I would rank with the very best 'short-lyric' poetry written during the last fifty years: *The force that through the green fuse drives the flower*, *Especially when the October wind*, *Why east wind chills*, *And death shall have no dominion*, *The Hunchback in the Park*, and *In my Craft or Sullen Art*. Over and above which there remains something like another twenty pieces of good, original, and largely lucid poetry. Upon such rough approximate accounting, can one arrive at any conclusion?

In his *New Bearings in English Poetry*, Dr. Leavis argues for the acceptance of Gerard Manley Hopkins as a major English poet. Without fully assenting to this evaluation, we cannot deny the key-position which Hopkins occupies in the history of modern verse. Now many critics have remarked Hopkins' influence on Thomas; and some would attribute to the latter a revitalisation of poetic language similar to that which

[7] I am aware of the strongly personal, and perhaps unshared, nature of this statement. There are some critics, I believe, who consider *A Winter's Tale* or *Vision and Prayer* as Thomas' best piece; and they are certainly striking poems. Then, too, the claims of such later poems as *In country sleep*, *Poem on his birthday*, and *In the white giant's thigh* will doubtlessly find strong defenders.

Hopkins effected. This, I believe, is to over-state the likeness, as well as to over-estimate Thomas.

D. S. Savage[8] has commented upon the "moral passivity" behind the poet's verse; and it is just this lack of tension (generated when an ethical passion clashes with a strong natural instinct) which limits Thomas' poetic vision. In all his work, there is nothing equal to the exaltation of *The Wreck of the Deutschland* or the inquisition of the 'terrible' sonnets. It is not with Hopkins that he must be compared.

The name of Gray, in this context, has been previously mentioned; and I think it is rather with such a poet that Thomas must be stationed. Gray's complete poetic work contains a little over half of the number of pieces included in Thomas' *Collected Poems*; and his fame rests on a mere handful of these: *The Elegy*, *The Bard* four of his six *Odes*, and possibly *The Progress of Poetry*. With this slender contribution, Gray helped to turn the taste of his age towards a warmer and more colourful style, and to free poetic language from the weary spell of Pope. The parallels with Thomas are not hard to seek; and if Thomas should prove equal to this measure, his fame and its longevity will be assured.

[8] See his essay on the poet in *Little Reviews Anthology 1947–1948*.

PART THREE

Prose and Drama

Prose

I

DURING THE COURSE of Thomas' career the writing of prose began to assume a greater significance as time went on. Starting from the seven stories in *The Map of Love* (1939), which may best be described as a poetic by-product, he progressed to the point where—according to Linden Huddlestone—"his hankering to develop his interest as a critic must not be forgotten".[1]

From early years he had done reviewing, namely, for the *Morning Post*, *New Verse*, and certain Welsh magazines and papers; but these labours, though well executed, he regarded in the light of bread-and-butter writing. His concern, therefore, in later days to express himself as a critic must be taken as having some meaning. Its import, I think, is that he was travelling to more objective modes of thought and composition. Now the purest of these are drama and criticism: the first, as the most imaginative; the second, as the most intellectual, form. That the only 'set piece' of criticism

---

[1] *Adam* no. 238, 1953. This is confirmed by E. F. Bozman in *Books* (Dec. 1953) where he observes that, at the time Thomas was writing the *Author's Prologue* to his *Collected Poems*, "he revealed to his publishers his intense interest in the stream of English poetry and his desire in years to come to work in the fields of criticism and analysis".

by him was a broadcast on the stories of Walter de la Mare, published in the symposium *Living Writers*,[2] in no way lessens the argument. A writer has only so much time at his disposal; and if he is predominantly creative, as Thomas most certainly was, then critical pronouncement and exposition—however fascinating it may prove—cannot hope to take first preference. Its claim is intriguing, but subsidiary.

If Thomas developed this latent stirring interest less than he might have done had he lived longer, the other pole of objective writing attracted him more and more. In drama, he put forth entirely new powers; and it might have seemed to many that his future lay in dramatic verse and prose than in personal lyrical poetry.

Part of his work in this medium began, indeed, in mercenary writing: his film commentary *Our Country*, written as propaganda during the war; the script for a film on oil, made in Persia; and other scripts for such films as *Three Weird Sisters* and *These are the Men*. That this task-work gave him the technique for more permanent dramatic productions—his scenario *The Doctor and the Devils* and the "Play for Voices", *Under Milk Wood*—need not be doubted.

But further examination of these two pieces belongs to the following chapter. Here, I want only to follow the development from the subjectivity of Thomas' early prose to the more objective mood of its later usage.

II

The seven stories in *The Map of Love* exhibit a typical young man's prose: not the prose of a young poet writing about poetry, but that of a poet using prose to convey what he has generally expressed in

[2] Edited by G. H. Phelps (Sylvan Press) 1947.

verse. (Remove the formal device of narrative and the tales in *The Map of Love* might all have been poems from that or previous volumes.) The value of these first stories, I should say, is that of Yeats' early stories. We read them, in retrospect, because they are the work of a fine poet, rather than because they succeed in themselves. But taken as a part of the poet's imaginary world, and read for the clues they offer to Thomas' literary temperament, and the confirmation of his mode of thought in verse, these tales are interesting enough. A second element in our just concern with them is that of their prophetic property—the way in which odd passages and phrases look forward to the objective consummation of the author's later prose.

The common quality in these seven stories is in the abnormal world they present. Some of them are fantasies; and others, while observing certain obligations to the claims of 'reality', make good their escape from such ties by employing themes of dementia and madness. The setting, in each case, is in Wales, within range of "the Jarvis Hills" (a fictional topographical reference). Most of the stories have pastoral backgrounds; though in one of them an industrial town is featured. But, unlike the later tales in *Portrait of the Artist as a Young Dog*, the *genius loci* or spirit of the place is only evoked in the most general terms. Place in these early stories is not a matter of particular locality but of vague associative ideas.

A word as to their themes and plots. In *The Visitor* a dying poet is visited each night by his friend Callaghan. One evening, Callaghan comes to him, takes him naked from his bed, and—carrying him in his arms—flies through the darkened countryside with him. In their flight the poet sees the processes of nature working. The terms of his vision are grand and amplified:

> The moon, doubling and redoubling the strength of her beams, lit up the barks and the roots and the branches of the

Jarvis trees, the busy lice in the wood, the shapes of the stones and the black ants travelling under them, the pebbles in the streams, the secret grass, the untiring death-worms under the blades.

Callaghan brings the poet back to his bed before the full breaking of the dawn. Rhianon the poet's wife "with a sweet, naked throat, stepped into the room.

> Rhianon, he said, hold my hand, Rhianon.
> She did not hear him, but stood over his bed and fixed him with an unbreakable sorrow.
> Hold my hand, he said. And then: Why are you putting the sheet over my face?

The figure of Callaghan (is he Death?) looks forward to "the Thief" in Thomas' poem *In country sleep*.

The Enemies tells the story of an old clergyman who loses his way in the hills. He comes to the house of a young couple, where he stays for a meal and a rest. The wife spends much time staring in the crystal, and the husband is engaged in a lasting war with the endless weeds of his fecund garden. Between them, they symbolise the powers of darkness—of occult 'pantheistic' forces. The man looks at the old clergyman and thinks, "He is afraid of the worm in the earth, of the copulation in the tree, of the living grease in the soil." The rector senses their pagan aura, and, feeling afraid, drops on his knees. "He stared and he prayed, like an old god beset by his enemies."

Anti-Christian, in another manner, is the parody of the Crucifixion in *The Tree*.[3] A pious elderly gardener

---

[3] Because the poet felt both attraction and repulsion for the teaching of the Church, it is hard to say how far such a story as this is 'anti-Christian' in intention. Indeed, the sympathy of the poet is clearly with the Christ-idiot figure, who is made to greet the boy as "Brother" as the wire cuts into his wrists. But the tale affects me as a travesty—a grim pathetic travesty, which replaces the story of the Crucifixion with a myth in which both parties are imbecilic.

tells a little lonely boy about the tree on which Christ was crucified. In the boy's mind the story grows confused; and at night he creeps out of his bed to kneel and pray at the tree's foot. On Christmas Day, an idiot, who has been roaming the countryside, is found by the boy sitting under the tree. The boy gets him to stand up and raise his arms, then secures him to the tree with wire from the potting-shed. After which, he returns with a handful of "silver nails".

The Map of Love relates how a boy and girl are initiated into the mystery of sex by the ghost of "mad Jarvis" and his many sweethearts. His voice cries out to them from all the fields in which he has prosecuted his many amours.

The Mouse and the Woman recounts the dreams of an inmate of a lunatic asylum; while in *The Dress*[4] an escaped lunatic (who has cut off his wife's lips because she smiled at other men) goes to sleep with his head in the lap of a terrified woman, into whose cottage he has broken.

The Orchards describes the dreams of the poet Marlais, in which he falls in love with a female scarecrow and her beautiful sister. One day, walking in the country, he meets the girl out of his dream, and sees that the scare-crow is also there. I do not know whether this story owes anything to Walter de la Mare's tale of the scare-crow, in some meadows beyond a lonely house, that approaches a little nearer each day.

In the main, literary influence in these stories seems small. It is possible, but unlikely, that the adventures of Michael Robertes, in the tales of Yeats, may have impressed Thomas; and the tales from *The Mabinogion* may have contributed a touch here and there.

---

[4] Because of my low estimation of the tales in *The Map of Love*, I think it only fair to remark that the fine short-storyist Glyn Jones considers *The Dress* to be "one of the most beautiful of modern short stories."

In his book *English Prose Style*, Sir Herbert Read has some remarks which help us to 'place' these seven stories. "Fantasy," he observes, "is a product of thought, Imagination of sensibility. If the thinking discursive mind turns to speculation, the result is Fantasy; if, however, the sensible, intuitive mind turns to speculation, the result is Imagination. Fantasy may be visionary, but it is cold and logical; Imagination is sensuous and instinctive." This, I think, serves to distinguish the processes by which Thomas produced his verse and early prose. In both cases, his subject-matter is the same. The 'pantheistic' "vegetable world", which "roared" under Mr. Owen's feet in *The Enemies*, is of the same universe as we encounter in Thomas' first two books of poems; but whereas the latter is the product of "the sensible, intuitive mind", the former has resulted from a lower-pressured "thinking". This may account for the "cold" unsubstantial quality of these tales which no show of rhetoric can hope to conceal.

But if the "Fantasy" of the seven tales does not succeed in creating the illusion of poetry, which it seems to wish to do, it fails also in achieving the element proper to its own genre—that "objectivity" which Sir Herbert Read posits as being its true distinguishing quality.

Disparate passages of 'poetical' musing or of too self-conscious prose, drift like mists through the stories, depriving them of narrative economy and shape.

Lacking a grasp of particulars as being part of a general body, these tales do, however, occasionally evince that celebration of individual traits, that closeness to things, which the later prose reveals. "Upon town pavements," Thomas writes in *The Orchards*, "he saw the woman step loose, her breasts firm under a coat on which the single hairs from old men's heads lay white on black." His perception here is as shrewd as that of Maupassant or the de Goncourts.

Anticipative, too, is the vivid use of the 'character' verb in the following sentence from *The Enemies*: "In her draughty kitchen Mrs. Owen grieved over the soup."

It is small points such as these that look forward to the pincer-like perception which we get in, say, *A Story* (1953): "The charabanc pulled up outside the Mountain Sheep, a small, unhappy public house with a thatched roof like a wig with ringworm."

III

Among other stories by Thomas which appeared about this time was one he contributed to *The New Apocalypse* (1939), a symposium of young writers. As this tale *The Burning Baby* was one which a number of people noticed, and as the group behind the anthology largely used the name and work of Thomas as sponsor and touchstone of their own movement, a few remarks may be devoted to it.

Revealing a greater flair for prose than any of the other tales in the volume, it has all the turgid morbidity —the pangs, and fits, and starts of a histrionic vision— which the work of the group as a whole displayed:

> They said that Rhys was burning his baby when a gorse bush broke into fire on the summit of the hill.

Spasmodically, though, the story manifests the inception of fresh prose qualities. There is the beginning of that humour which plays so large a part in Thomas' later stories. As yet, it shows itself concerned with obscene features or symptoms of decay—a kind of joyless Rabelaisianism:

> He took his daughter's hand as she lay in the garden hammock, and told her that he loved her. He told her that she

was more beautiful than her dead mother. Her hair smelt of mice, her teeth came over her lip, and the lids of her eyes were red and wet.

or

Rhys Rhys sat in his study, the stem of his pipe stuck between his fly-buttons, the bible unopened on his knees.

or consider the sadism of the tale's last paragraph:

And the baby caught fire. The flames curled round its mouth and blew upon the shrinking gums. Flame round its red cord lapped its little belly till the raw flesh fell upon the heather. A flame touched its tongue. Eeeeeh, cried the burning baby, and the illuminated hill replied.

Judged as a Gothic extravaganza in the manner of Matthew Lewis' *The Monk*, *The Burning Baby* must be said to succeed; but success in so specious a category as this is no solid proof of literary distinction.

The three chapters of Thomas' uncompleted novel *Adventures in the Skin Trade*[5] belongs to 1941, and later; and so represent more recent work than the stories in his book *Portrait of the Artist as a Young Dog* which was first published in 1940. I prefer, however, to take the former first, since, genuinely entertaining as these chapters are, they do not display the 'vintage' qualities present in the earlier volume.

Adventures in the Skin Trade is an amusing fragment—a prologue to a sort of picaresque novel, in which the hero is a young provincial who entrains for London to seek for fame and women. Reading it, I was reminded of how Henry Miller said he went to Paris "to study vice". The twenty-year-old Samuel Bennet of the *Adventures* resorts to the metropolis for much the same purpose; but in the author's account of his quest there is none of that "dead-pan' earnestness of Miller, for whom

[5] Chapter one first appeared in *Folios of New Writing* no. 5 (Autumn, 1941); Chapters one and two (with the first section of Chapter one missing) in *Adam* no. 238 (1953); and Chapters one and two complete in *New World Writing* no. 2 (U.S.A.).

the affairs of sex, one feels, are a Germanic substitute for philosophy. His adolescent aspirations of a somewhat disreputable nature are described with buoyancy, with a sympathetic spiritedness which does not exclude fun at the hero's expense. In fact, the wishes of the young poet (Samuel Bennet is clearly an alias for Thomas) to be thought a practised whoremonger, when he is as virgin as makes no difference, are mercilessly made the most of. Leering at a woman in the buffet at Paddington whom he assumes to be a prostitute (she smells, he decides, "of eau de cologne and powder and bed"), he succeeds only in being cold-shouldered, and in getting his little finger stuck in the neck of a Bass bottle. Befriended by an odd furniture-dealer, he is taken to a near-by café, where a plain nymphomaniac with glasses escorts him upstairs to the bathroom to ease the bottle from his finger with soap. She finally gets him naked in the bath, makes him drink a glassful of Cologne, and then climbs in on top of him[5a]. When he regains his mental composure, he sees the furniture-dealer and a friend standing by the bath considering him: the bottle is still on his little finger.

Shivering in the unwarmed water of the bath, as he waits in the darkened room for the girl to step in with him, the young man's thoughts are taken up, half with the natural fears of his situation and half with revenging himself on the far suburb that bore him:

> Come and have a look at impotent Samuel Bennet from Mortimer Street off Stanley's Grove trembling to death in a cold bath in the dark near Paddington Station.

The earlier part of this fragmentary novel describes the young man leaving home and his journey up in the train. During the night before his departure he

[5a] It is hard to say what, if anything, takes place. Indeed, from the story it is by no means certain that the girl *does* climb in. Perhaps this was part of Thomas' joke (on the basis of one type of *risqué* story which follows suspense with an anticlimax.)

creeps downstairs and does a lot of damage so that he can "never come back". He draws rude shapes on his father's papers, tears up the family photos, and breaks his mother's best china:

> A tureen cover dropped from his hand and smashed.
>
> He waited for the sound of his mother waking. No one stirred upstairs. 'Tinker did it', he said aloud [Tinker is the family pom], but the harsh noise of his voice drove him back into silence.

The gestures, the poses, the unconscious humour, and the grief of late adolescence are all here:

> He burnt the edge of his mother's sunshade at the gas mantle, and felt the tears running down his cheeks and dropping on to his pyjama collar. Even in the moment of his guilt and shame, he remembered to put out his tongue and taste the track of his tears. Still crying, he said, "It's salt. It's very salt. Just like in my poems. "

Sitting in the lavatory in the London train, he completes the process of burning his boats which he began earlier at home. From his note-book he tears out and destroys the names and addresses of people he can use as introductions to publishers and editors, leaving only the name and phone-number of a street-girl he has never met.

One sees that Samuel Bennet is quite set on "doing the Rimbaud" (as Thomas so well expresses it else-where); but unlike the French poet or his fictional counter-parts (Lafcadio, say, in André Gide's novel *Les Caves du Vatican*), there is no innocent belief behind this young man in a 'pure' cult of evil. Samuel Bennet would, no doubt, like to be wicked, and tries very hard to be so; but his youth and experience keep changing his audacities into bathos. It is this maturity of mind in Thomas, at back of his hatred of convention, which preserves a sense of proportion in its most corrective form: self-critical humour.

Since I have spoken in this high fashion of *Adventures in the Skin Trade*, and yet suggested that we shall not find the 'vintage' prose of Thomas here, it behoves me to give my reasons. The lack resides, I think, in his character-drawing. Samuel Bennet, his parents, and sister are well shown; but the off-setting group of bohemian figures, which the young man encounters in London, are rather too much to type. The character known as Mr. Allingham is something of an exception. A furniture-dealer who lives in a flat so fantastically crammed with his purchases that he has no room to turn round, and yet is furiously annoyed at the suggestion that the world is not sane, he has some of the Dickensian colour which Thomas gives to his later characters. On the other hand, the characters of George Ring (a poetry-loving pansy), Mrs. Dacey, and Polly have but small fetching likeness about them.

IV

Portrait of the Artist as a Young Dog, a 'touched-up' and thinly-veiled autobiography, consisting of ten stories, is a gem of humorous juvenile frankness. Allowing for its more disruptive plan, the book possesses a vivid truth similar to that of *Huckleberry Finn*. It has poetry, humour, psychological shrewdness, and an excellent swiftness in character-depiction.

In the description of farm-life and the country (see *The Peaches* and *A Visit to Grandpa's*) there are passages that prompt us to compare this aspect of Thomas with Alain-Fournier. Both have a like prose lyricism, and a kind of youthful nostalgia; but the Frenchman is more naively idealistic and sentimental than Thomas, and has not got his anodyne of humour.

Another comparison, or contrast perhaps, is to be found in the 'William Brown' stories by Richmal Crompton. But the "I", the narrator in the *Portrait* (which commences with his adventures as a small child to the time when he becomes a junior reporter) begins where the popular figure leaves off. For the conventional 'naughtiness' of William (smashing a pane of 'old Jones' ' green-house with his catapult or ball), Thomas substitutes a quite unbowdlerised catalogue of delinquencies:

> I let Edgar Reynolds be whipped because I had taken his homework; I stole from my mother's bag; I stole from Gwyneth's bag; I stole twelve books in three visits from the library, and threw them away in the park; I drank a cup of my water to see what it tasted like; I beat a dog with a stick so that it would roll over and lick my hand afterwards; I looked with Dan Jones through the keyhole while his maid had a bath; I cut my knee with a penknife, and put the blood on my hand-kerchief and said it had come out of my ears so that I could pretend I was ill and frighten my mother; I pulled my trousers down and showed Jack Williams; I saw Billy Jones beat a pigeon to death with a fire-shovel, and laughed and got sick; Cedric Williams and I broke into Mrs. Samuel's house and poured ink over the bedclothes.

In place of the young 'doctored' protagonist—the prig disguised as a ragamuffin—which Richmal Cromp-ton offers us, we have a real *enfant terrible*, a quite irrepressible junior Titan thirsting for the blood of all experience.

We see him, in *Patricia, Edith and Arnold*, playing-up the house-maid and listening to her talk; scrapping with a school-boy who becomes his best friend, and with whom he exchanges fantasies of future artistic greatness (in *The Fight*); pursuing, unsuccessfully, the caresses of school-girls (in *Extraordinary Little Cough*); getting drunk in the sailors' pubs as a 'cub' reporter (in *Old Garbo*); and just missing a love-experience with a beautiful young street-walker (in *One Warm Saturday*).

But the various phases of growth through which the youthful hero passes are counter-parted, as it were, by the diversity of the book's other characters: foxy

"Uncle Jim", in the course of trading his live-stock over the counter for liquor; cousin Gwilym, training for the ministry, who writes poems to actresses, practises his sermons from a cart in the barn, and masturbates himself in the farm privy while reading pornographic books; "Grandpa" who lights his pipe beneath the blankets, and sits up in bed driving imaginary horses; the drunk man who lost most of his posterior in a pit-accident (for which mischance he was awarded "Four and three! Two and three ha'pence a cheek"); the old begger who removes his cap and sets his hair on fire for a penny ("only a trick to amuse the boys", scornfully observes the young narrator)—these, and many others, vivify the *Portrait*.

And, in this book, we have proceeded from the half-mythical landscapes of *The Map of Love* to a real particularised Welsh world; not so compact and concentrated as that of Thomas' dramatic literature, yet still singularly present before the eyes. The optic nerve, on the watch for those individual splashes in the palette of local colour, vibrates finely in these stories:

> The rain had stopped and High Street shone. Walking on the tram-lines, a neat man held his banner high and prominently feared the Lord.
>
> *(Old Garbo)*

In all, this book evinces a closer direction of language over and above that of the first short stories. The elimination of marginal terms—of words that do not hit the bull's-eye of their object—is apparent if we take a passage from both books. Here is a specimen from *The Map of Love*:

> But there had been no woman in his dream. Not even a thread of a woman's hair had dangled from the sky. God had come down in a cloud and the cloud had changed to a snake's nest. Foul hissing of snakes had suggested the sound of water, and he had been drowned. Down and down he had fallen, under green shiftings and the bubbles that fishes blew from

their mouths, down and down on to the bony floors of the sea.

(The Mouse and The Woman).

and here a passage from the *Portrait*:

> Night was properly down on us now. The wind changed. Thin rain began. The sands themselves went out. We stood in the scooped, windy room of the arch, listening to the noises from the muffled town, a goods train shunting, a siren in the docks, the hoarse trams in the streets far behind, one bark of a dog, unplaceable sounds, iron being beaten, the distant creaking of wood, doors slamming from where there were no houses, an engine coughing like a sheep on a hill.
>
> *(Just like little dogs).*

How subtly, and truly, the words "unplaceable sounds" have been inserted in this exact catalogue of auditory impressions! Without them, the precision would have been unreal.

But the whittling accuracy of Thomas' thought behind his choice of terms is best demonstrated in the placing of one word:

> Uncle Jim [seated in his trap], in his black market suit with a stiff white shirt and no collar, loud new boots, and a plaid cap, creaked and climbed down.

Another author might well have written, ". . . climbed down, creaking", thus losing the exact connotation. The creaking preceded the climbing down, and was not simultaneous with it—the sound being caused by "Uncle Jim's" preliminary movements as he raised himself from a sitting position. With the one particular verb, in its particular place, Thomas conveys this straightaway.

Since the *Portrait* Thomas wrote a number of other stories and sketches in which the evocative use of language and the condensing of impressions were further developed. These later pieces, together with other prose-writings not published before in book-form, are appearing in the winter of this year with Messrs. Dent, under the title of *Early one Morning*.

Drama

I

FROM THE PROSE- to the dramatic-work of Thomas, we pass by natural transition. The conversational passages in the *Portrait* and the *Adventures* were lively and in keeping with the speakers; and, in one or two instances (cousin Gwilym in *The Peaches*, the drunk man in *One Warm Saturday*, and Mr. Allingham in the *Adventures*) vividly idiosyncratic.

With Thomas' growing interest in people, and the flagging of the lyrical subjective spirit in him, it was proper that the drama should prove his next stage. From the stories it could be seen that a larger scope for spoken speech was required by him. It was clear that, with his ear for language, Thomas could do more with dialogue if he had the broader, more appropriate framework. That framework he found in dramatic writing: the film scenario of *The Doctor and the Devils* and "A Play for Voices" *Under Milk Wood*.[1]

I find this trend of thought confirmed by what the poet's friend, Daniel Jones (who wrote the music for *Under Milk Wood*) has to say in the play's preface. "The publication," he writes, "of Thomas' *Collected Poems* in 1952 marked the end of one period of his literary development;[2] after this according to his own

---

[1] As published in book-form by Messrs. Dent (1954).

[2] Philip Burton, who contributed a reminiscence of the poet to *Adam* no. 238 (1953) supports this. Just before Thomas left for America on his last voyage, he discussed with him his dramatic plans for the future. "Hindsight wisdom", writes Mr. Burton, "inevitably gives an added depth to some

words, he intended to turn from the strictly personal kind of poetry to a more public form of expression, and to large-scale dramatic works in particular, where there would be scope for all his versatility, for his gifts of humour and characterization as well as his genius for poetry."

In the chapter on Thomas' last poems, I spoke of their 'Virgilian' quality, of the large and luminous acceptance of the world which they express, along with a cessation of the self-explorative urge in the poet. Now just this aspect, which did not bode well for the continued working of the lyrical poet, was favourable to the dramatist in Thomas. A lyrical poet needs to look inwards, a dramatist outwards, on the world. For the latter there must be some few things held in common, a certain *status quo* visible to all, a dramatic gravity exerted on everyone. Without this sense of a shared world for a stage, there can only be the collision of isolated beings—microcosm bumping up against microcosm without any converse or recognition.

Acceptance of life, then, and the impression that acceptance brings knowledge of what it is all about, is as good for the dramatist as it may be stultifying for the lyrical poet. One of Thomas' commentators[3] has remarked how in the early poem *Especially when the October wind*, "the poet first fully assumed his Orphic role, celebrating a particular day, a particular place." This role was often overlaid by Thomas' poetry of private enquiry; but in the stories, and finally in drama, it asserts itself in increasing splendour. Just as *18 Poems* is a landmark to adolescent isolation, so *Under Milk Wood* is a lasting monument to the world of adult

of the things that Dylan said that evening, but it is now clear to me that he felt he was coming to the end of his first lyrical impulse. He talked with affectionate warmth of a new poem he had written about his father, and talked as though it was likely to be the last of its kind."

[3] W. S. Merwin in *Adam* no. 238 (1953).

community. And writing, as he does of parish happenings, the poet's language loses its cloudy probing. Powerfully experimental as it remains, the speech of this "Play for Voices" is common speech, a racy Anglo-Welsh utterance amplified out of dialect into a vivid mundane poetry. In embracing the vision of 'otherness', the language of Thomas has attained the public register.

Before considering his two dramatic works—*The Doctor and the Devils* and *Under Milk Wood*—I feel I should add a rider to a statement I made in the chapter on Thomas' last poems. There, I remarked that this phase of his poetry exhibited every excellence save that of conceiving something new. In the light of what the poet told his friend Daniel Jones—that he was turning from private poetry—perhaps my observation holds. But the power of conceiving and doing something new, which I think was passing from Thomas in the realm of lyrical poetry, does not apply to his dramatic writing; since the canons for these two media are different. For a lyrical poet, 'the power of conceiving something new' is that of expressing an original emotional vision of the world. For the dramatist, it is that of creating a fresh concourse of characters and situations. This power is abundantly shown in Thomas' two dramatic pieces.

II

The first of these was the screen-play *The Doctor and the Devils* (1953), taken from a story-line by Donald Taylor, and based on the murders of Burke and Hare. In an appendix, Mr. Taylor tells us that "The screen-play of *The Doctor and the Devils* is the first to be published as a book before the film has been produced. This is no doubt due to the literary quality, unusual in this medium."

His statement prompts us to consider the function of words in screen-plays in general. Obviously enough, the use of words in such a dramatic composition is twofold: first, to provide the characters with dialogue, or such monologue as may be given to them; and, secondly, to describe the scene, the background to the action, and the action itself, as it results from the movement of the characters. This second purpose encompasses all that is known to film-personnel as the 'shooting directions'; and it is chiefly in the need for fulness of statement or suggestion that the screen-play differs from the script of a drama intended for the stage.

It might be thought that the 'shooting directions' entail too precise instructions to the camera for there to be any scope left for literature—the human and aesthetic exposition of the scene. This, however, is not the case, a screen-play not being primarily a technical document; but (outside the dialogue) a sort of essay in suggestion. In his appendix to *The Doctor and the Devils*, Mr. Taylor informs us that "The most satisfying and commercially successful films have a background of idea which is the driving force behind the plot. . . . It is insufficient in making any film to have a good plot, if there is no basic motive behind it. The screen-play of *The Doctor and the Devils* was written because I had been searching for some years to find a story that would pose the question of 'the ends justifying the means'."

This concerns what we may call the psychological heart of the piece; but another aspect, as important as this, is the atmospheric unity or consistency. The first property is one that the screen-play shares with any mode of dramatic art; but the second belongs peculiarly to cinematic expression. The reason for this is, that the old 'unities of time and place' never applied to film creation. It is true that in a Chekov play, there is a likeness of psychological tone, a common resonance throughout, so to speak; but this atmospheric unity depends largely on the characters, and only—to a small extent—on the scene. With the usual limitation of a stage-play to three acts, the scenic effects are circumscribed. In a screen-play, this is otherwise. The scene may change as many times as the author pleases; and, with the technique of 'close-ups' and 'long-shots', the number of variations upon one scene, one place, are infinite.

And this variety, this richness, has all to be expressed in visual terms: ultimately, by camera-work; but, originally, by language which conveys the visual effects to be produced. It is here that the screen-play writer needs to be something of a descriptive artist; and, if he can forget his rhyme and metre, it is better still if he is a visual-minded poet.

But there is a further consideration binding on the screen-play writer. This artist in impressions, appearances, superfices, must know how to make consistent the multiplicity of all that he sees. Remarking on the nature of much "impressionistic writing" in his own day, Arthur Symons once complained that "all is broken, jagged, troubled in this restless search after the broken and jagged outlines of things. It is all little bits of the world seen without atmosphere."[4]

This statement holds in solution the *sine qua non* of descriptive screen-play writing: the plurality of impressions must be referred to one atmospheric constant. More than half the merit of *The Doctor and the Devils* comes from Thomas' achievement of this. The first 'shot' of the film illustrates this process.

All the 'notes' or images of the play, which are to be developed later, are present in this opening: the loneliness, arrogance, and intellectual eminence of Dr. Rock, the Gothic confusion of the city (reminiscent

[4] *Dramatis Personae* (1925).

of Meryon's sky-scapes of Paris) with its suggestion of misery and poverty ("top-heavy tenements, hovels, cottages, pigsties"); and the clash or crossing of these two elements—contemptuous knowledge and vicious illiteracy.

And this data is given us not by statement but by symbol. Dr. Rock's compelling powers of mind are presented to us through his "stick" which he wields "like a prophet's staff", and his irrepressible application in "the insatiable, and even predatory, curiosity of the bent-forward head". Then, too, the rumour of guilt or sin, of tragic pride or fate, is communicated by our first sight of the Doctor as "A small black figure with another darkness billowing around it", which later becomes that of "a youngish man in severe professional black", the "darkness" about him revealing itself as his "long cloak". The whole presents a rather Mephistophelean image.

In the screen-play's opening scene, the implications of the man and the city, interpreted through visual counters, are conveyed together. From now on, we shall see them developed, for the most part, separately; but their joint or juxtaposed appearance at the beginning is imperative, since it is from the contact of two worlds—that of well-fed intellectual aristocracy and that of vicious besotted penury—that the tragedy is to spring.

The atmosphere that unifies these two separate spheres is one of caricature, of exaggeration. Both in the 'low-life' figures of this screen-play and in its characters from the drawing-room, a Dickensian spirit prevails. The presentation, in both cases, owes much to conventions of melodrama; but, here, it is a kind of melodrama in which the sinister is tempered by the facetious and grotesque. This, for instance, is how Thomas shows us a trio of body-snatchers, from whom the future murders, Fallon and Broom, get the idea:

"INTERIOR OF A TAVERN.

On a bench in a corner sit three men. No one sits next to them, though the tavern is crowded. We recognise them as the three men of the graveyard. All three are drunk, though solemnly as befits men whose business is death.

The very tall top-hatted man (Andrew Merry-Lees) is a cadaverous clown; a deacon of the drinking-cellar, a pillar of unrespectability.

The other top-hatted man (Praying Howard) has an almost benevolent, almost sweet and saintly, appearance run to seed and whisky.

The short man (Mole) is very hairy; almost furry, like a mole.

They raise their tankards to each other.

ANDREW MERRY-LEES: To the dead!

PRAYING HOWARD: To the Surgeons of our City!

And when we come to Dr. Rock's world, there is the same heightened note, the same stepped-up presentation. Shot 29 shows us "the students in the LECTURE HALL OF DR. ROCK'S ACADEMY.

"Rock enters.

He enters like a great actor; he acknowledges the ovation of his audience; he bows; he steps to the platform table; he adjusts his spectacles and his cuffs; every movement is studied."

Again, we are given the stature of Dr. Rock in the conversation of his younger colleagues; and even this oblique account observes the same high-mannered pitch:

"HARDING: . . . How did the dinner go?

MURRAY: Thomas [Rock] was on top of the world.

BROWN: Gracious, loquacious, insulting, exulting. . . .

HARDING: [Overtopping him] . . . drastic, bombastic, charming, disarming.

BROWN: [Not to be outdone, with extravagant gestures] . . . avuncular, carbuncular.

HARDING: What did he talk about at dinner, apart from sex and religion and politics?

MURRAY: Body-snatchers."

The last word links the two worlds of the play.

Broom and Fallon, the murderers, who kill their victims before they sell their corpses to Dr. Rock for the purpose of dissection, are chiefly delineated, in visual terms, by their actions. Broom is described as "dog-haired". We see him leaping on to a barrow, which his slatternly woman is wheeling.

Earlier, in a tavern-scene, we see him "crackling his way through the crowd, jumping and finger-snapping, a long damp leer stuck on the side of his face." Drinking with Fallon and their women, he seizes Nelly's tankard. "Nelly makes to snatch the tankard back, but Broom suddenly shows his teeth and pretends to snap at her." The words which the characters speak are often no more than clarifying compliments to their actions, as when Kate says to Nelly: "Ach, leave him be. Broom's got the devil in him to-night. He'd bite your hand through. I know him."

This visualising of the characters, even so far as concerns their inner life, is a proof of just how far Thomas has borne his new medium in mind. When applied to such elementary and elemental types as Fallon and Broom, it seems entirely justified. Fallon, sitting drunk in a tavern, looking, terrified, at his strangler's hands, asserting that "there's devils in them" and that those he has killed were "my brothers . . . and my sisters . . . and my mother . . .", speaks primarily through his movements, through the stillness and twitching of his hands. Indeed, there is only one passage in which the words of these 'low life' figures tells us more than their own actions or settings. This is after Fallon's last murder, when he stands at the window of the lodging-house, looking out on the heavily falling snow:

"FALLON: It's cold in hell to-day.
The fires are out.

Nelly looks at him in uncomprehending silence.

FALLON: Nothing can burn me any more.

I'm a cold man, Nelly.

I'm numb all over, like an old dead finger-nail.

No more dancing.

No more drinking and singing.

But the method of presenting character by its out-ward physical symptoms—appropriate to such animal types as the two murderers—has certain disadvantages when dealing with more evolved personalities. From Donald Taylor's appendix to the screen-play, we know that the tale of Dr. Rock "was written because [he] had been searching for some years to find a story that could pose the question of 'the ends justifying the means'" In other words, the originator of the play which Thomas wrote intended that the piece should be moral drama or tug-of-war with conscience, as well as a crime-and-detection story.

That Thomas in his screen-play failed completely to convey this—and failed because he found no way of representing inwardness of character—is obvious. Never, until the last scene, after the trial of the two murderers and his own public disgrace, is Dr. Rock shown as entertaining any qualms concerning the source of the bodies that are sold to him for purpose of autopsy. The only value he recognises is that of disinterested scientific research; and morality is con-founded in his mind with all that is entailed by respec-tability. His attitude to ethical issues, as others see them, is one of arrogance. Outside of that which promotes research, he accepts no claims or checks upon his conduct: he is very much the Nietzschean super-man. There is none of that questioning and wrestling with conscience which we might expect the protagonist of a play treating of 'ends and means' to reveal. Right up to Dr. Rock's last monologue, we believe that the tragedy of the piece (in so far as it refers to the Doctor)

is that of the great man punished for his pride, for the
sin of *hubris* which the Greeks spoke of. Then we see
that, after all, the struggle of the conscience was
supposed to be embodied. As he meditates upon his
career, and his fall from public esteem, we hear the
Doctor's voice:

> "And the child in the cold runs away from my name. . . .
>   My name is a ghost to frighten children. . . .
>   Did I *know*, did I *know* from the very beginning?
>   Never answer, never answer, even to yourself alone in the
> night. . . .
> All's over now. . . .
> Oh, Elizabeth, hold my hand. . . .
> 'Oh, it isn't a hand, it's a pair of scissors! . . .'
> Did I set myself up as a little god over death?
> Over death. . . .
> All over . . . over . . . over. . . .
> Did I set myself above pity? . . .
> *Oh, my God, I knew what I was doing*! "

"Did I *know*, did I *know* from the very beginning?"
and "*Oh, my God, I knew what I was doing*!"—two lines
in the whole play, the only two that indicate the
struggle we are to suppose has gone on! It winds things
up and makes for an effect, but psychologically is a
poor crude gesture. No doubt, as a species of film-
writing, it compares very favourably with similar
concluding passages, but as a piece of drama intent on
representing the truth of human nature it is both
shoddy and specious.

Part of Thomas' failure here seems to derive from
his exclusive use of the visualising process to indicate
the thoughts and feelings of his characters. To express
the inner life of Broom and Fallon in gestures and
actions, rather than in words, was an entirely satisfactory resolve; but the higher complex nature of the
Doctor's personality required more elaborate presentation: either a number of finer traits and gestures which
should symbolise the workings of his will and his

conscience, or words which in some way should suggest the direction of the conflict within him. Because Thomas provided neither of these, the figure of the Doctor remains something of a Byronic 'dummy' for all the energy of rhetoric which he tries to pump into him.

To find what is positive in *The Doctor and the Devils*, we must look at it not as high tragedy, but as a dramatic description of poverty and crime on a clearly lower level, artistically speaking. The whole richness of the story adheres to its treatment of the world of 'low life'. The upper level of Edinburgh—the professional academic world of Dr. Rock—is tamely depicted in comparison.

The grim humour—of paradox and contrast—is present in Thomas' painting of the sordid slum backgrounds. Broom and Fallon live in "Rag-and-Bone Alley":

In a first-floor window hangs a sign:

CLEAN BEDS

Kate opens the door and goes through. Fallon follows her. Broom leaps from the barrow and is inside the dark door-way like a weasel into a hole."

The humorous implication here is excellent: the tenement, with the sign CLEAN BEDS in the window, is really a weasel's hole.

Humour is present, too, in much of what Broom and Fallon say; as in their remarks on an old man, who has died one night at their lodging-house:

BROOM: Hammer him in, hammer him in. Four pounds rent all dead in a box.

FALLON: Now who would have thought old Daniel could be so mean: Dying without a word, and owing us four pounds. He didn't even have a penny piece hidden under the straw
. . . .

BROOM: If only he was alive again so that I could kill him with my hands. . . .[5]

FALLON: And all he left was a bit of a broken pipe. . . . And livin' here all these months on the fat of the land. . . . Many's the night I've beaten the rats off him myself. . . ."

This is the environment of Charles Dickens—the Dickens inspired, as he often was, by Mayhew's world of the London poor, but described with a naked cynicism of speech foreign to the nineteenth-century author. The talk of the 'sub-men' Fallon and Broom establishes almost a new category of the facetious; at the same time, degraded, poetic, and horrific. One is convinced and made cold by these rogues because they go naturally about their crimes, with so easy, unconspiratorial a bearing.

But the verisimilitude and success of the world of 'low life' in this play is not complemented by Thomas' treatment of the upper-middle-class world of Dr. Rock. These spheres are hemispheres which do not properly fit.

And as to the "background of idea which is the driving force behind the plot" ("the question of 'the ends justifying the means'"), the play does not happily or truly possess it. Its strong point is background of atmosphere.

III

If the grotesquerie of Dickens is observable in *The Doctor and the Devils*, then a broader, more general, element of the novelist informs the "Play for Voices" *Under Milk Wood*; namely, his exuberance. In describ-

[5] It is not quite clear from the text whether the old man died a natural death, or whether he was the first of the murderers' victims. Broom and Fallon speak their words in front of a carpenter, who has been called in to nail the old man into his coffin. Broom's wish that he was alive again "so that I could kill him with my hands" may therefore have added ironical meaning.

ing the surface tics of character, the visible oddities of individual difference, *Under Milk Wood* is truly Pickwickian. And, as with the *Pickwick Papers*, what we remember is not plot but portraiture, not the actions of people but the people who commit them.

In one point, though, the likeness breaks down. For all their robustious extrovert existence, the characters of Dickens have a certain reticence. Their observance of Victorian sexual proprieties is exemplary enough to point to inhibition. Whenever Mrs. Grundy might be offended, the assertive current that feeds their lives becomes tame, conventional, effete. There is, of course, no question of keeping the bridle on Thomas' creations. The denizens of *Under Milk Wood* are Dickensian figures with the blinkers off. The erotic for them is a spur, not a bit. They are not, like characters from Dickens, real figures too frequently flawed with a paste-board front or a card-board facet: one feels they are flesh and blood throughout. Thus, Gossamer Beynon, "demure and proud and school-marm in her crisp flower dress and sun-defying hat, with never a look or lilt or wriggle", tells herself, concerning an undeclared admirer, "I don't care if he *is* common. . . . I want to gobble him up. I don't care if he *does* drop his aitches . . . so long as he's all cucumber and hooves". And this irrepressible frankness informs the self-confession of most of the characters.

Sometimes this takes the form of dream-thoughts or day-dreams, of memories (as Captain Cat's of Rosie Propert), or of songs put into the character's mouths but meant as only audible to the inner ear (Polly Garter's song and that of Mr. Waldo).

Under Milk Wood is described as "A Play for Voices". This phrase primarily refers to the play's suitability for broadcasting; but it may be as well to consider more closely the specific nature of the work. Now if we begin by defining a drama as a form of stage narrative possessed of a *dénouement*, it will be hard to allow that *Under Milk Wood* is a drama at all. Like James Joyce's *Ulysses*, the form this work of Thomas takes is cyclic: an account of twenty-four hours of life in the little fishing-town of Llaregyb. But, unlike Joyce's novel, there is no hero—no Bloom or Stephan—and no substantial accession of self-knowledge to any of the characters, in *Under Milk Wood*. As things have been, so they go on: the 'bad' characters (Nogood Boyo, Polly Garter, and Mr. Waldo) remain 'bad', and the 'good' characters (the Rev. Eli Jenkins and Miss Myfanwy Price) remain 'good'. There are no conversions and no retrogressions; for vice and virtue, in this work, are seen only as attributes of individuality, like winking, stammering, or jerking one's head.

This is not to say that the play does not contain a number of incidents and situation, a variety of limited dramas *in petto*. But the sum of these incidents cannot be expressed in a formula common to them all. They are just so many daily actions and intentions of separate people living in the same town. So Polly Garter continues to enjoy the intimate male company of all and sundry, Dai Bread the baker to share his two wives, Mog Edwards to woo Miss Myfanwy Price, Mr. Pugh to plan to poison Mrs. Pugh, and Mr. Waldo to drink and whore with the same alacrity as ever.

The actions, then, in *Under Milk Wood* are episodic rather than dramatic. They illustrate the nature of the characters, not in the changing fitful light of time but rather *sub specie aeternitatis*. In this sense, the characters of *Under Milk Wood* are static unephemeral creations. Their author has so fallen in love with the uniqueness of their individual make-ups that he has chosen to celebrate them by giving them a type of permanent existence. This permanence bears some relation to that which Keats intended in his *Ode on a Grecian Urn*.

Llaregyb, the town in Thomas' play, is like Keats' "unravished bride of quietness": time cannot terminate the actions which take place there. But the actions are not, as in the poem, of an idealised nature. Instead of the happy piper, the lover and his girl, and the priest leading the heifer to the sacrificial altar, we have the acid bickerings of Mr. and Mrs. Pugh, the house-proud severities of Mrs. Ogmore-Pritchard, the crazy inanities of Lord Cut-Glass, and a dozen other brands of small-town boorishness. And yet, because of this un-ideal existence, the appearance of reality is the greater. Thomas has somehow learned to look at the mundane and the ordinary with such a fund of love, that the celebration of their most indifferent points has become a matter of great moment to him. He has desired to perpetuate their memory as the average man desires only to perpetuate the memory of exceptional things.

Perhaps with my talk of the 'ordinary' and 'mundane', I may have given the impression that Thomas has employed a naturalistic approach—a restrained objective noting of detail in an almost scientific spirit. This is far from being the case. The style and presentation of *Under Milk Wood* belongs to the realm of heightened realism, of lyrical caricature, which Thomas had started to use in the 'low life' scenes of *The Doctor and the Devils*. The pervading air of lyricism is established by the descriptive passages spoken by the 'two voices', which act as commentators. Their utterances constitute a breathless condensed kind of prose-poetry with many colloquial over-tones:

"FIRST VOICE (Very softly)

To begin at the beginning:
It is spring, moonless night in the small town, starless and bible-black, the cobblestreets silent and the hunched, courters'-and-rabbits' wood limping invisible down to the sloe-black, slow, black, crowblack, fishing-boat-bobbing sea.

The strong evocative power of this passage derives from the same method as that of Whitman's poetry: its charm is the charm of accumulation—the recital of an inventory of objects. But the literal fascination of this list is strengthened by certain literary devices: by long dexterous trains of adjectives, by transferred epithets, and the use of the *mot juste*. The sea, for example, is conjured up by preceding a mention of it with five attributes ("the sloeblack, slow, black, crowblack, fishing-boat-bobbing sea"); and in another passage in the play a noun has six adjectives before it ("the slow deep salt and silent black, bandaged night").

Association, as well as definition, plays a large part in the language here: the "dingles" in which the moles play by night are described by the word "snouting", and the "yards" in which the dogs sleep are spoken of as "wetnosed".

And as for the exact term, the precisely delineating reference, the passage contains instance after instance: "*bible-black*" night, "*dumbfound* town", "*webfoot* cockle-women", "*tidy* wives", "*anthracite* statues of horses" in the dark.

The essence of this 'catalogue' poetry is seen in another passage in which twelve nouns follow one another: "Only you can hear and see, behind the eyes of the sleepers, the movements and countries and mazes and colours and dismays and rainbows and tunes and wishes and flight and fall and despairs and big seas of their dreams."

It is this vivid processional quality of words which provides the atmospheric background to the play. On the whole, it is an admirable device, a potent conjurative force; but there are occasions on which its use becomes a little monotonous. The syntax of the sentences in these background pieces is too often cut to a pattern; and though the choice of diction is excellent, the arrangement of the words tends to be repetitive. But it is only a minor criticism, and the fault could easily be remedied by shortening or omitting some of the commentaries spoken by the 'two voices'.

I have said that these passages of recitative, by the two commentators, provide the atmosphere to the entire play; but it would be quite wrong to think of that atmosphere as exclusively poetic in the elevated sense. Some of the passages are humorous in spirit, with the humour that belongs to the eccentricly absurd:

> "FIRST VOICE
>
> Jack Black prepares once more to meet his Satan in the Wood. He grinds his night-teeth, closes his eyes, climbs into his religious trousers, their flies sewn up with cobbler's thread, and pads out, torched and bibled, grimly, joyfully, into the already sinning dusk."

With its natural speech-rhythms, the language of the characters provides a counter-point to the more literary idiom of the 'background' commentators. And humour (often unintentional from the speakers' point of view) is the chief element in what they have to say. One of Thomas' methods here is to construct a dialogue out of a string of conversational clichés, as in the little shorthand epitome of scandal concerning Mrs. Waldo and her trial of a husband.

When there comes a need to express themselves more deeply, the characters resort to songs; as Polly Garter does when she sings about her first sweetheart, "little Willy Wee who is dead, dead, dead". These songs serve to acquaint us both with the life-stories of the singers, and the reason why they are such people as they are. Polly Garter's song, then, is an apologia for her as a wanton: the death of her first lover turned her that way:

> But I always think as we tumble into bed
> Of little Willy Wee who is dead, dead, dead.

Similarly, listening to Mr. Waldo's song, we understand why he behaves like the profligate that he is:

> In Pembroke City when I was young
> I lived by the Castle Keep
> Sixpence a week was my wages
> For working for the chimbley sweep.

Hardly a favourable start in life!

The Rev. Eli Jenkins, for his part, unburdens his heart in his poems: all the soft, sentimental, optimistic goodness of the man is in them: sincere, kindly, mediocre, imitative.

The song-game of the children coming out of school is one of the finest pieces of the play. The ruthless cruel innocence of childhood is splendidly portrayed in the hard-and-fast rules with which they conduct their forfeit game. Whether Thomas invented this ritual for himself or whether he took it from some local or traditional children's song, it remains a brilliant realistic image of the juvenile world by an adult.

We have seen how *Under Milk Wood* lacks certain qualities properly associated with drama how time in this play is not progressive but cyclic; and how vice and virtue, good and evil, are seen only as personal properties (adornments, one might almost say), and not as psychological or spiritual determinants.

Because of these aspects, *Under Milk Wood* is best considered as a pageant play, a parochial pageant play with dialogue, rather than as a more normal kind of a drama. Into this static time-free world, where action is not subject to ethical judgment in the form of some visiting nemesis, grief and mortality hardly enter. But, here and there, rumours of their workings intrude; and, though these cannot be said to impart a dramatic constitution to the play, they heighten its latent poetry and intensify our sense of the real.

Polly Garter's song, first sung complete and then
heard with variations in snatches, haunts us with its
nostalgic conclusion; just as Captain Cat's commun-
ing with his memory of Rosie Probert haunts us with
its unforgetting passion. From "the bedroom of her
dust", Rosie speaks to the Captain in a passage of
great pathos:

> "Remember her.
> She is forgetting.
> The earth which filled her mouth
> Is vanishing from her.
> Remember me.
> I have forgotten you.
> I am going into the darkness of the darkness for ever.
> I have forgotten that I was ever born."

The utter renunciation of death reverberates in these
lines as it does in the ballad of *The Unquiet Grave*:

> "'Tis down in yonder garden green,
>   Love, where we used to walk;
> The finest flower that ere was seen
>   Is withered to a stalk.
>
> "The stalk is withered dry, my love,
>   So will our hearts decay;
> So make yourself content, my love,
>   Till God call you away!"
>
> O wet and weary is the night,
>   And even down pours the rain, O.
> And he that was sae true to me
>   Lies in the greenwood slain, O.

But such plangencies as these, by their unquenchable
melancholy, serve to make more real and piquant the
gay acceptance of life as a whole, which *Under Milk
Wood* magnificently expresses. Without some suggestion of *lacrimae rerum*, 'the tears in things' of which
Virgil speaks, laughter is no more than an idiot's

cackle or the tedious exertion of a commercial 'funster'. It is not without significance that Shakespeare's Falstaff becomes, in part two of *Henry IV*, so genuinely pathetic a figure.

Yet, all in all, *Under Milk Wood* is the gladdest thing that Thomas ever wrote. In the words of one of his own characters, "It is Spring in Llaregyb in the sun in my old age, and this is the Chosen Land". In this work, Thomas has found the Chosen Land which every artist looks for: release from one's own private obsessions and complete absorption in the outside world. Here, for the first time on such a scale, our most private of private poets speaks out largely, for all to hear, with a resounding intelligible voice.

In a note to his *Collected Poems*, Thomas told us that the contents were written "for the love of Man and in praise of God". Even more do these sentiments apply to *Under Milk Wood*—a kind of dramatic anthem praising the uniqueness of all created matter.

No more than *The Doctor and the Devils* can this play be considered as high drama. Unlike the former, though, *Under Milk Wood* clearly had no pretensions in that direction. What it intended, it achieved; and that achievement (though not properly dramatic) was as new and vital and excellent in itself as anything written for literary broadcasting during the last twenty-five years.

PART FOUR

A Literary Post-Mortem

I

MORE THAN TEN YEARS have now elapsed since Dylan Thomas left us. Since that time no writer of verse with so intense an aura, or *mana,* has arisen. In Britain the poetic scene is hardly ablaze with major luminaries. T. S. Eliot's long silence as a *poet*[1] is to be expected on account of his age. We are not the men the Victorians were, going down vaticinating to the grave.

Only one figure of high imaginative stature has addressed himself to poetry readers since Thomas' decease in 1953—the Orcadian poet Edwin Muir who died himself in 1958. Since then, poetry has been in the hands of a

---

[1] In an early essay on poetic drama, Mr. Eliot argued that the poetry and the drama were one. Such does not seem to be the case in his recent 'West End comedy' plays. *The Cocktail Party, The Confidential Clerk* and *The Elder Statesman* quite consciously stress the distance between the poetry and the drama, with the poetry dropping unashamedly behind. For the intellectual light of these plays, their sober wit, and grave serenity, we should be—in this age of trifling—truly grateful. But we have only to compare these three works with Thomas' *Under Milk Wood* to feel their 'stripped' quality—their winter barrenness as to 'dancing' words. *Under Milk Wood*—a broadcast play, is, of course, no *drama*, in an Aristotelian sense. There is no real 'beginning, middle and end' about it. Its form is circular, without resolution. It all takes place in 'Country Heaven.' "As it was in the beginning, is now, and ever shall be: world without end. Amen." Dramatically, the play does not leave the starting-post, but in *living language, memorable speech,* it makes us feel how verbally severe, how strict and 'ungladsome' is the Eliot trilogy.

number of neo-academics—plain men professing some small feats of learning—the 'University wits' belonging to 'the Movement': John Wain, Kingsley Amis, Donald Davie, Elizabeth Jennings, Philip Larkin, John Holloway, and others.[2]

The poetry written by these is a "small hard and dry" sort of utterance. It is often ingenious, sometimes amusing, occasionally pretentious, and generally on the defensive. Much of it is honest respectable work, though nothing to make a song and dance about. The forces of fashionable criticism in Britain have attempted to bolster these minor virtues, presenting them as natural voices off-setting the stridency of earlier rhetoric. Philip Larkin's poem *Church Going,* a little masterpiece of precise pedestrianism,[3] has been held to justify the new lower plane, the common ground level of the wingless English Muse. To critics abroad, this lack of elevation seems less a matter for gratulation. For Professor Rosenthal, an American authority, the much-prized Larkin is no plain man's phoenix. Larkin, he remarks, "is for ever promising to be a wit and then appealing to the reader to pity him instead"[4]—a 'hard' poet with a soft centre.

This brief summary of minority 'minor voices' is a somewhat necessary digression. 'Bashing the Forties' has been a part of the critical programme of the 'Movement' poets; and Thomas as the fourth decade's most volcanic poet has received a fair share of the mud which has been flung.

For the third time running Oxford has elected a real live writer of verse to fill her Chair of Poetry. In Robert Graves she has chosen an original and salty talent, a poet with a clean cutting edge to his mind. As Oxford Professors of

---

[2] See the anthology *New Voices,* edited by Robert Conquest.
[3] This is not intended as a pejorative but as a descriptive remark.
[4] v. *The Modern Poets: A Critical Introduction.*

Poetry go, the University could not have done better.[5] But
Graves, for all his Irish blood, his humour and fantasy,[6]
regards Thomas with classical disapproval which he has
expressed with Celtic picturesqueness. In his Clark Lectures, *The Crowning Privilege,* he speaks of the poet as
concealing "a defect in sincerity" by introducing "a dis-
tractive element." "He keeps musical control of the readers
without troubling about the sense."

Thomas' star is too intense a body to be quenched by
unfavourable fashionable opinion, but it is clearly not in
the ascendant with the controlling coteries of taste. It is
rather with 'the common reader', 'the poetry lover', that
his fame remains safe.

II

Thomas' status, to-day, is somewhat curious. He is, at
once, one of the most widely-read modern poets, while
being out of fashion with the avant-garde élite.

In an excellent essay in his volume *Vision and Rhetoric,*
G. S. Fraser[7] characterized the change that had come over
English poetry in the fifties. It represented, as he put it,
a triumph of the pedant over the bohemian. The new poet
was academically-minded. Thomas was bohemian and so
was 'out'.

One of the aspects of this anti-bohemianism was that
the 'cult of personality'—sometimes to be found in the
post-Romantic poet—was now studiously frowned upon.
As a spokesman of the new self-denying ordinance, Donald

[5] The other candidates for the Chair (Enid Starkie, Helen Gardiner,
and F. R. Leavis) were known as scholars and critics, not as poets.
T. S. Eliot declined to stand, and John Betjeman said he had nothing
to say.
[6] See, for example, his poem *Welsh Incident* in which humour and
fantasy are combinedly present.
[7] G. S. Fraser is one of the few illuminating and balanced critics who
have written on Thomas since the poet's death. There is a monograph
on Thomas by him in the *Writers and Their Work* series, sponsored by
the British Council.

Davie, remarked that what we wanted was not poets but poetry: the sacred waters, not the mere vessel. It was James Mitchie, I remember, who provoked Mr. Davie to this stern distinction. Writing of Thomas' death, Mr. Mitchie had remarked that "the gloom it caused was almost patriotic". "Dylan," he wrote, "was a figure, a character, a bard, even a card; he looked and behaved more like a poet than anyone since Yeats. Whatever our ideas may be about the artist's place or responsibility in society, we all cherish archetypal pictures of the Poet just as we do of the King. We may have monarchs who behave and dress like us, or slightly better; we may have forced them democratically to do it; but half of us wants the bold, bad, gorgeous kings and queens back again. It's the same with our poets. They may disguise themselves protectively as business-men nowadays, but is this what the public really wants? Dylan was wild and generous, flamboyant, unpredictable, religious, ribald, and thirsty. His poetry was rhapsodical, anti-industrial, and, above all, musical."

Poetry must at all times be at war with the Philistine spirit; but there is no guarantee that a personal bohemianism implies the presence of a producing poet. The flowing locks, the aggressive tie, the magniloquent manner of speech, and the *panache:* these would sometimes seem to be offered as poetic substitutes, an ersatz art.

Looked at in this light, Mr. Davie's grey rebuke to all the lamenting Dionysian voices, raised at Thomas' passing, was just. The only test of a poet's work is in his poems, line for line. Even so, a poet's personality, exhibited *outside* his verse, can still tell us much about his work— helping us, possibly, to bring it into focus. Any poem, in the end, must stand on its own feet (or be dismissed for its failure to do so). At the same time, no poem exists in a vacuum. It manifests itself in a personal context—as a 'note' or feature of someone's existence.

Thomas' biographical features *do* supplement his poems.

And the strange harmony consisting of his life and his poetry help to explain the real and diffused sense of grief at his death.

Thomas *looked*[8] like a poet, *sounded* like a poet, and wrote like a poet. Self and *persona* came together to produce an over-all bardic impression. When Thomas died, then, it seemed to many people as if the spirit of poetry died also. Never had such a rumpus been created in the Press since the passing of Tennyson and Swinburne. But whereas both of these were old men, Thomas was still in his middle prime—at least as far as years were concerned. "The death of a young poet," writes Karl Shapiro in *Dylan Thomas: The Legend and the Poet*,[9] "inflicts a psychic wound upon the world." Thomas' life, his poetry, and his death, maintains Shapiro, "touched the raw nerve of the world . . . and keeps us [still] singing with pain." This is the sort of language which Mr. Davie objected to, yet Mr. Shapiro's contention is abundantly borne out by John Malcolm Brinnin's book *Dylan Thomas in America* (1956).

"The poetry of Thomas," continues Shapiro, "is full of the deepest pain; there are few moments of relief. What is the secret of his pain-filled audience?" The answer he gives is that the poet wrote his own Adonis-myth. "Thomas," he maintains, "was the first modern romantic you could put your finger on, the first whose journeys and itineraries became part of his own mythology, the first who offered himself up as a public sacrifice. Hence the piercing sacrificial note in his poetry, the uncontainable voice, the drifting almost ectoplasmic character of the

[8] The most haunting likeness to the poet I know is a photograph reproduced in *Vogue* which showed Thomas standing knee-deep in leaves in a sunken tomb in a Welsh churchyard. Here we have a physical image of the elegiac poet of *Fern Hill*, *The White Giant's Thigh*, and *Poem on his Birthday*.
[9] "A collection of biographical and critical essays" edited by E. W. Tedlock (1960).

man, the desperate clinging to a few drifting spars of literary convention."

Shapiro's appreciation, if correct, would provide us with a clue to Thomas' deep hold on the contemporary public. By far the greater part of our major modern art is filled with the shivering apprehension of mortality; and Thomas not only expressed this in his verse, he lived it out on the stage of existence.

"I shall be dead within two years, drinking, exploring, going to the devil," Thomas declared when he was twenty-one. Those two years turned out to be eighteen, but the same burden of doom, imminent or to come, sounds throughout all phases of his work: "I see you boys any summer in your ruin" (from *18 poems*) is one with "The voyage to ruin I must run" contained in the last pages of the *Collected Poems*. And in between these is *Twenty-four years* (from *The Map of Love*) with the image of the poet "crouched like a tailor" in the groin of the natural doorway:

> Sewing a shroud for a journey
> By the light of the man-eating sun.

"Dressed to die," the poet of this poem is one with "the cureless counted body" of *Deaths and Entrances*.

By June 1952, John Malcolm Brinnin had come to the conclusion that Thomas' "unhappiness lay in the conviction that his creative powers were failing, that in his great work he had moved from 'darkness into some measure of light' . . . but now that he had arrived, he was without the creative resources to maintain and expand his position. As a consequence, he saw his success as fraudulent and himself as an impostor."

From this terrifying self-knowledge he retreated into the amnesia of drink.

When he returned from these phases of compulsive oblivion, the daylight was harsh. He knew he was sentenced—sentenced by his own hand. The shock of recognition was too great—and he would retreat into drinking again. The pressure which led him to play the alcoholic ostrich to the point of tragedy can best be suggested in the following passage. Fatally sick on his last American tour he confessed his fears to Herb Hannum, an architect friend, as reported by Brinnin:

"I guess I just forgot to sleep and eat for too long" [he told Hannum after being taken ill at a rehearsal of *Under Milk Wood*]. "I'll have to give up something." "What do you mean, Dylan?" asked Herb, "do you mean life?" "No," Dylan said soberly, "I don't know . . . I want to go on . . . but I don't know. I don't know if I can. I don't feel able any more. Without my health I'm frightened. I can't explain it. It's something I don't know about. I never felt this way before and it scares me. When I was waiting for the plane this time in London, I found I was drinking in a mad hurry . . . like a fool, good God, one after another whisky, and there was no hurry at all . . . I had all the time in the world to wait, but I was drinking as though there wasn't much time left for me . . . to drink or wait. I was shocked . . . I felt as though something in me wanted to explode, it was just as though I were going to burst. I got on the plane and watched my watch, got drunk, and stayed frightened all the way here . . . really only a little booze on the plane but mostly frightened and sick with the thought of death. I felt as sick as death all the way over. I know I've had a lot of things wrong with my body lately, especially the past year or so. Since I was thirty-five I've felt myself getting harder to heal. I've been warned by doctors about me, but I could never really believe them . . . that I was ever sick seriously or in any real danger. I didn't know how to believe it . . . or maybe I did believe it, but couldn't accept it. I think I just felt that I might be getting old faster than I expected to, older than I should be at my age. But now I don't know. Maybe I've always been frightened but didn't know it until I couldn't drink when I wanted to."

"Maybe I've always been frightened but I didn't know it"—all of Thomas' terrified wonder in the face of life *as he saw it,* is present in this statement. Earlier he had told a loyal woman friend that "the worst horror in life," "the horror beyond horrors, was the sense of being hopelessly trapped." One day later he was telling her of his "feelings of dread . . . a terrible pressure—as if there were an iron band round my skull."

Thomas was well and truly trapped. The Dionysian was indeed brought low. "I can't do anything any more," he said. "I'm too tired to do anything. I can't ——, I can't eat, I can't drink . . . I'm even too tired to sleep."

III

Such was the experiential background to Thomas' later poetry. This was poetry quite consciously written "As I sail out to die." From the same poem *In Country Sleep,* we can draw his image of self-recognition: "one man through his sundered hulks." One of his own "boys of summer in their ruin" he had come, with fearful logic, to manhood's full estate.

Behind all Thomas' poetry there lies a limited pantheism—an intense and terrible vision of the world as subject to the law of diminishing returns. It was stated simply, at the off-set, in that famous piece from *18 Poems:*

> *The force that through the green fuse drives the flower*
> *Drives my greenage; that blasts the roots of trees,*
> *Is my destroyer.*

Coupled with this pantheism of Thomas, there went a kind of physical determinism. There is no free-will in Thomas' world; only the brute unreason of drives and instincts working out their course. In Thomas' work sex

knows no choice. His early story *The Burning Baby* plots
the graph of an incestuous relationship in which a father
lies with his daughter who afterwards dies in child-bed.
The father, a minister, takes the off-spring and burns it
on a pyre on a high hill in Wales. The tale is a Gothic
horror-piece, written perhaps with the poet's tongue just
a little in his cheek, but the predestined path of events, in
all its naked unalterability, is what the story expresses.
The Reverend Rhys Rhys knows the evil of his action,
both before and after it has been committed. He even
preached a sermon in his church on the very eve of sleeping with his daughter, against the sins and lusts of the
flesh. But knowledge and judgment are no check against
the 'conditioned' urges of his blood.

The characters in Thomas' work are like Pavlov's dogs:
there is no *will* in them, their behaviour being by reflexes.
Just like Little Dogs, a later story, presents us with the
same theme, namely that of man conditioned and imprisoned by his response to stimuli. The two characters in the
story have both ruined their lives by lying with girls they
were not in love with, and this immediately after making
love to girls for whom they felt a deeper attraction. "Just
like little dogs" are the magistrate's words in making out
a maintenance order against the fathers. They are trapped
by their rutting doggishness, by a bitch-like nature per-
petually on heat. Man's sexual life, in Thomas' poems, is
expressed in terms of animal metaphors. The lover and
seducer of women is represented as a "hickory bull", "a
flailing calf or cat in a flame", and lastly as "a black sheep
with a crumpled horn". Nature in Thomas is unredeemed.
It is adamant in its insistent expression. The poet's pantheism is not a-moral—it is 'guilty' and 'unrecovered' by
grace.

In Thomas' 'guilty pantheism', then, there is no final
notion of salvation. All that can be promised is immortality—the life-urge which possesses one form leaves it but

lives on in another. So Thomas, in his poem *And Death shall have no dominion* interprets St. Paul's text in his own heretic fashion: "Heads of the characters hammer through daisies", "though loves die love shall not"—we are re-incarnated and inherit a fresh species.

The limitation of Thomas' viewpoint both for life and poetry is seen in his own tragic self-destruction. There was no hard moral core to it, and without some view-of-life which could free his moral will he was destined to end, in total exhaustion—the law of diminishing returns had its way.

One can, if one wishes, picture his existence as being like that of the beautiful young men chosen for sacrifice to ancient Aztec gods. For a period before the sacrifice, the Adonis-figure was garlanded and fêted. The finest food and drink, the most lovely girls, were freely offered him: at the end came the knife.

Thomas, likewise, advanced through life as a celebrant who knows the end is in store for him. His poetic life was a kind of debate between lament and exultation. It was when the vein of celebration ran dry that he knew his appointed time had arrived. Celebration and lament reach their utmost joint expression in *Poem on his Birthday*, his deepest excursion into self-knowledge. Here he writes of how "He celebrates and spurns / His driftwood thirty-fifth wind turned age"; of how "Thirty-five bells sing struck / On skull and scar where his loves lie wrecked"; of "The voyage to ruin I must run." Yet throughout all this lament, it is celebration which has the last word:

> *the closer I move*
> *To death, one man through his sundered hulks,*
> *The louder the sun blooms*
> *And the tusked, ramshackling sea exults.*

Here it is death itself he celebrates; and in this act he passes the test of the highest romantic poetry. One can perhaps compare the approach of 'romantic' and 'classical' poetry in this matter by contrasting Keats' *Ode to the Nightingale* with T. S. Eliot's *Ash Wednesday*. Keats, half "in love with easeful death", in the agony of his love for Fanny Brawne, dreams of ceasing "on the midnight with no pain". Barred from full physical expression of his love, Keats finds a sort of consummation in the thought of fading and vanishing away:

> Fade far away, dissolve, and quite forget
>   What thou among the leaves hast never known,
> The weariness, the fever, and the fret
>   Here, where men sit and hear each other groan;
> Where palsy shakes a few, sad, last gray hairs,
>   Where youth grows pale, and spectre-thin, and dies;
>   Where but to think is to be full of sorrow
>   And leaden-eyed despair;
> Where Beauty cannot keep her lustrous eyes,
>   Or new Love pine at them beyond to-morrow.

His imagined loss of identity in the darkness of the night is a substitute for the lover's "little death" which he has had to forego. Death, or annihilation, is seen as a final positive. This orgasmic sense of the void, this last release into non-existence which the 'romantic' poet sometimes welcomes is unacceptable to the classic writer. For him, it is all too 'mystical', too spiritually vague and 'pantheistic'. Thus, T. S. Eliot, in *Ash Wednesday*, faced with the knowledge that he may no more drink: "There, where trees flower, and springs flow, for there is nothing again" —that "the one veritable transitory power" is denied him, rejoices not in thoughts of annihilation but in the more difficult prospect of

> having to construct something
> Upon which to rejoice.

From this point onwards, Eliot was emotionally committed to the life of religion. Thomas, too, possessed a religious sense, but asking for no 'proofs', no certitudes, no intellectual 'prints' (as Eliot did), he was content to express these 'veerings', these stirrings of the mind, in less fixed fashion.

As I said before, praise and lamentation sound alternately throughout the poem. Like Lawrence's *The Ship of Death, Poem on his Birthday* is not a conclusion, a finis or finale, psychologically speaking. It is not the tale of a dead-end destination so much as a log of discovery, a song of exploration rather than exhaustion. One way of putting it would be to say: The end is come, but the best is not yet. This, then, is the context in which Thomas places statements of a highly ambiguous order. These lines are particularly relevant:

> And to-morrow weeps in a blind cage
>   Terror will rage apart
> Before chains break to a hammer flame
>   And love unbolts the dark
>
>   And freely he goes lost
> In the unknown, famous light of great
>   And fabulous, dear God.
>
> Dark is a way and light is a place,
>   Heaven that never was
> Nor will be ever is always true,
>   And, in that brambled void,
> Plenty as blackberries in the woods
>   The dead grow for His joy.
>
>   There he might wander bare
> With the spirits of the horseshoe bay
>   Or the stars' seashore dead,
> Marrow of eagles, the roots of whales
>   And wishbones of wild geese,
> With blessed, unborn God and His Ghost,
>   And every soul His priest, . . .

Here we encounter a God who is "dear" yet somehow "fabulous" and "unborn", and a heaven which is referred to as a place "that never was / Nor will be ever" yet is, at the same time, "always true". What can we make of these paradoxes? Are they anything but self-contradictions.

By concentrating on one term at a time, it might be possible to build up a full meaning. Thus we might say that when Thomas speaks of God as "dear" he is thinking of the desirability of the notion of deity, and that "dear" also carries with it a sense of intimacy, a reference to someone emotionally near at hand. When we pass on to the term "fabulous", all the affirmative vibrations of the first word are lost. But "fabulous" need not be taken as synonymous with "unbelievable". Its suggestion here may rather be "that which appears as highly strange or fantastic to the undiluted rational mind." A third connotation is "that which belongs to the nature of the fable rather than to the more prosaic narrative." So far, we see there is no essential contradiction in the spirit of the passage. Nor need the term "unborn" disturb us. God is spoken of as "unborn" possibly because a faith in Him, a feeling of certitude concerning His existence, has not yet been born in the poet. If this is so, the term is subjective, and in no way denies God's objective being. Heaven "that never was / Nor will be ever" and yet is "always true" presents at first glance a harder problem. One reading of the sense, however, may be that heaven whose reality has always existed bears no resemblance to what man has believed, or now believes, its nature to be. The truth of its existence, in other words, must be taken in conjunction with the falsehood of all our notions of it.

This is one way—a pan-Christian way—of interpreting this poetic puzzle; but to me the kind of statements Thomas makes here seem rather to invite comparison with the celebrated *mot* which parodies, yet serves to summarize, Santayana's thinking: "There is no God, and Mary is His Mother." I mention Santayana's name on purpose. In his book *Animal Scepticism and Faith,* he describes himself as being "an ignorant man, almost a poet." When a philosopher, however ironically, can humble himself in this fashion, his words may assist us in understanding the self-subsistent undefining images of art.

A passage from Santayana's Preface may help us to view the enigma of Thomas in an unusually fruitful fashion. "I lay siege," he writes,

to truth only as animal exploration and fancy may do so, first from one quarter and then from another, expecting the reality to be not simpler than my experience of it, but far more extensive and complex. I stand in philosophy exactly where I stand in daily life; I should not be honest otherwise. I accept the same miscellaneous witnesses, bow to the same obvious facts, make conjectures no less instinctively, and admit the same encircling ignorance.

Santayana is saying that his philosophy is not all of one piece in the sense, for example, of a straight length of string. The thoughts that feed it do not come blowing single-mindedly from one direction. Instead, the "miscellaneous witnesses" which go to make up his picture of things are met with first in one quarter, then another. Nor does he pretend that his self-patterned world has the validity of a cosmic blueprint or of a map metaphysically to scale. "My system," he frankly admits, "is no system of the universe."

Santayana likewise provides a useful lead-in to Thomas when he draws a distinction between moral and animal faith. The latter he describes as "a sort of expectation or openmouthedness," while "when a man believes in another man's thoughts and feelings, his faith," he tells us, "is moral, not animal." It would be interesting to compare this distinction between moral and animal faith with that which the Roman Catholic church establishes between acquired and infused knowledge: acquired knowledge being that which the church teaches, infused knowledge that which God plants in us. Now those who submit to the Christian faith have generally expressed their sense of infused knowledge, at least partly, in terms of knowledge acquired. But if we say that Thomas' poetic intuition represents a kind of infused knowledge, then this is just what he does not do. His faith being of an animal order, he did not believe he should express it in terms of "another man's thoughts and feelings." And because, as Santayana tells us, animal faith is "a sort of . . . open-mouthedness," he expresses both his negative and positive reactions to the thought of deity and after-existence: "blessed, unborn God and His Ghost," "fabulous, dear God," "Heaven that never was / Nor will be ever is always true."

We have become accustomed to hearing poetry spoken of as the language of paradox. Thomas is not a metaphysical poet in the sense we allow to Donne or Eliot. Intellectual curiosity, a mental passion in dealing with ideas play little part in his poetry. What we *do* have, rather, in his verse are the warring sentiments at play within us. God—though *felt* to be unbelievable ("fabulous")—is none the less "dear". The *sentiment of a belief* remains on after the disappearance of intellectual dogmatic conviction. Similarly—though no show is made of establishing the truth of denial—the sentiment of doubt is expressed in the poetry. And these two feelings fuse together in a poetic clinch which makes for paradox.

Thomas is interesting as a poet of religious temperament nourished in a literary culture of doubt.[10] Certitude, proof, or commitment have no part in his thinking. He is the agnostic who has retained a naturally religious imagination.

---

[10] It is interesting to compare Thomas' *Poem on his Birthday* with Philip Larkin's *Church-Going*. Larkin, as a poet, is an agnostic who has *not* retained a religious imagination. What Larkin finds impressive about the church in this poem is not any notion of it as having supernatural implication. He sees it, and respects it, only as a repository of serious moral ideas and strivings. Larkin interprets the word *God* as an archaic reference to 'goodness'. What interests Thomas in the notion of God is not His goodness but His glory.

IV

In his fascinating "historical grammar of poetic myth"[11] Robert Graves distinguishes between two main types of poetry. The romantic poet, he tells us, is the 'Muse-Poet'— his verse is, *au fond,* an address and homage to the Moon- or Woman-Goddess. His work is rhapsodic, a-rational, 'matriarchal'. Opposed to poetry of this order is the work of the 'classical' poet. His approach is 'Apollonian'. His symbol of reverence is the Sun God; and his verse dedicated to reason and knowledge. His vision of society is 'patriarchal'. He is, *par excellence,* the scholar-poet.

These are large, loose terms to make free play with; but perhaps they do suggest some basic distinction. Thomas is clearly not of the second order. He is no scholar-poet as Jonson was, as Dryden after him, or later still Arnold. But can he be said to answer to the particularized description of the Muse-Poet?[12] Thomas is rhapsodic, a-rational and committed. He writes from the mid-stream of experience without practising a detachment from it. If his poetry is not "simple", at least it is "passionate and sensuous."[13] There is also something esoteric in his verse—the suggestion of an occult rite, of something celebrated at a secret shrine.

All this would show Thomas as possessed of Muse-Poet attributes . . . but for one significant fact. The Muse-poet, according to Mr. Graves, writes poetry of homage. The figure who receives this homage is the White Goddess, or Ideal Woman.[14] In Thomas, we shall find no trace of this imaginative chivalry. Women, in Thomas' plays and stories, are no better than they should be:

[11] *The White Goddess.*

[12] Mr. Graves strictly considers Thomas no true poet at all, or as a poet of "promise", not "performance."

[13] Milton was clearly a scholar-poet, but his famous statement of poetry's triple virtues describes more fully the Muse-Poet's work.

[14] The one ideal feminine figure in Thomas' poetry is, significantly, not quite a woman but the she-bird in *A Winter's Tale.*

fallible, weak, or wanton. Woman, in his verse, is anonymous and faceless—a sort of sub-human Venus Pandemos. Thomas, then, is a Muse-Poet, but his homage is offered to the 'Life-force', not the Woman.

English poetry in the 'Forties' was clearly marked by Muse-Poet values. In the 'Fifties', the prevailing values of judgment were those of the Scholar-Poet. Under this late régime in fashion, Thomas' rating has declined. One is reminded of the young Mr. Eliot's greater interest in Jonson over Shakespeare. Thomas, like Shakespeare, is not a 'safe' model; but a poet's verse may have another function than that of providing a workshop for the tyro. It may have something to say to the mere reader—the common reader—who finds in it delight.

Selected Bibliography

The following list makes no claim to being either detailed or complete. A full bibliography is being prepared by Mr. J. Alexander Rolph, which Messrs. Dent are publishing.

I

WORKS BY DYLAN THOMAS

(a)

Books

18 Poems (Parton Press, republished by Fortune Press) 1934.
25 Poems (Dent) 1936.
The Map of Love (Dent) 1939.
The World I Breathe (New Directions, U.S.A.) 1940.
Portrait of the Artist as a Young Dog (Dent) 1940.
New Poems (New Directions, U.S.A.) 1942.
Deaths and Entrances (Dent) 1946.
The Selected Works of Dylan Thomas (New Directions, U.S.A.) 1946.
In country sleep (New Directions, U.S.A.) 1951.
Collected Poems 1934—1952 (Dent) 1953.
The Doctor and the Devils (Dent) 1953.
Under Milk Wood (Dent) 1954.
**Early One Morning* (Dent).

> *At the date when this bibliography went to press, the contents of the above title had not finally been determined; nor had a publication date been scheduled. I was thus unable to indicate which of the following magazine contributions (I*b*) are to be considered as included in it.

(b)

Miscellaneous works published in magazines

Answer to an Enquiry (*New Verse*, no. 11) October 1934.
A Fine Beginning (*New Writing*, no. 5) Autumn 1941.
Our Country (*Wales*) Autumn 1943.
Quite Early One Morning (*Wales*) Autumn 1946.
Holiday Memory (*The Listener*) November 1946.
Memories of Christmas (*Wales*) Winter 1946.
The Crumbs of One Man's Year (*The Listener*) January 1947.
Conversation about Christmas (*Picture Post*) December 1947.
How to be a Poet, I & II (*Circus*) April and May 1950.
The Followers (*World Review*) October 1952.
Adventures in the Skin Trade (*New World Writing*, U.S.A.) 1952.
Four Lost Souls—second part of the above (ibid.) 1953.
   [both parts of the above are republished—with one abbreviation in *Adam* no. 238, 1953.]
A Story (*The Listener*) September, 1953.
A Visit to America (*The Listener*) April 22, 1954.

(c)

Stories and essays contributed to anthologies

The Burning Baby: first published in *Contemporary Poetry and Prose*, reprinted in *The New Apocalypse* (Fortune Press), 1939.
A broadcast on the stories of Walter de la Mare, published in *Living Writers* (Sylvan Press), 1947.

II

WORKS ON DYLAN THOMAS

(a)

Books and pamphlets

Marshall W. Stearns: *Unsex the Skeleton—Notes on the Poetry of Dylan Thomas* (first published in *Sewanee Review*, and later reprinted—with some omission—in *Transformation* no. 3, 1946) 1944.
Henry Treece: *Dylan Thomas* (Lindsay Drummond & Benn) 1949.
Roger Asselineau: *Dylan Thomas* (*Etudes Anglaises*, Paris) January 1954.

(b)

Chapters and passages in books and anthologies

Francis Scarfe: *Dylan Thomas; a Pioneer* in *Auden and After* (Routledge) 1942.
J. L. Sweeney: Introduction to the *Selected Works of Dylan Thomas* (New Directions, U.S.A.) 1946.
Cecil Day Lewis: *The Poetic Image* pp. 122–128 (Cape) 1947.
Geoffrey Grigson: *How much me now your acrobatics amaze* in *The Harp of Aeolus* (Routledge) 1947.
D. S. Savage: *Dylan Thomas* in *Little Reviews Anthology 1947–48* (Eyre & Spottiswoode) 1948.
Noel A. Jones: *Dylan Thomas as a Pattern* in *British Annual of Literature* vol. 6, 1949.
Lawrence Durrell: *Key to Modern Poetry* pp. 196–199 (Peter Nevill) 1952.

(c)

Relevant articles in magazines and reviews

Glyn Lewis: *Some Aspects of Anglo-Welsh Literature* (*Welsh Review*) 1946.
William Kean Seymour (unsigned): *Poets and Pretenders* pp. 128–129 (*Poetry Review*) April–May 1946.
Wolf Mankowitz: *Dylan Thomas* (*Scrutiny*) Summer, 1946.
M. Williams: *Welsh Voices in the Short Story* (Welsh Review) 1947.
William Empson: *How to Understand a Modern Poem* (*Strand*) March 1947.
Dr. Edith Sitwell: *Comment on Dylan Thomas* (*The Critic*) Autumn 1947.
Henry Gibson: *A Comment* (*The Critic*) Autumn 1947.
Stephen Spender: *Poetry for Poetry's Sake* (*Horizon* no. 76) 1947.
Tambimuttu: *Eleventh Letter* (*Poetry London*) September–October, 1947.
Hardiman Scott: *From Death to Entrance* (*Outposts* no. 7), 1947.
Aneurin Rhys: *Dylan Thomas—A Further Estimate* (*Poetry Review*) April–May 1948.
Geoffrey Grigson: *Correspondence* (*Poetry London*) June–July 1948.
Tambimuttu: *Correspondence* (*Poetry London*) June–July 1948.

Linden Huddlestone: *An Approach to Dylan Thomas* (*New Writing* no. 35) 1948.

Nicholas Moore: *The Poetry of Dylan Thomas* (*Poetry Quarterly*) Winter 1948.

Glyn Lewis: *Dylan Thomas* (*Welsh Review*) Winter, 1948.

R. G. Cox: *The Cult of Dylan Thomas* (*Scrutiny*) September, 1949.

Harvey Breit: *Talk with Dylan Thomas* (*New York Times Book Review*) May 14, 1950.

David Alvarez: *The Poetry of Dylan Thomas* (*Hudson Review*) Autumn 1950.

John Pudney: *Wales Loses a Great Poet* (*Picture Post*) November 1953.

E. Bozman: *Dylan Thomas* (*Books*) December 1953.

Stephen Spender: *Dylan Thomas* (*Britain To-day*) January 1954.

Dr. Edith Sitwell: *Dylan Thomas* (*The Atlantic*, U.S.A.) February 1954.

John Davenport: *Dylan Thomas* (*Twentieth Century*) December 1953.

James Mitchie: *Correspondence* (*The London Magazine*) February 1954.

Donald Davie: *Correspondence* (*The London Magazine*) March 1954.

Raymond Garlick: *The Endless Breviary* (*The Month*) March 1954

(d)

Magazines devoting all or some of their pages to articles, reminiscences and poems upon Dylan Thomas. The contributors and their contributions are too numerous to list here

Adam nos. 237 and 238, 1953.

Encounter December, 1953 and January, 1954.

Dock Leaves (Pembroke Dock, Pembroke) Spring, 1954.

Addendum.

In between the writing and the publication of this work there appeared a new book on the poet: *The Poetry of Dylan Thomas* by Elder Olson, (University of Chicago Press,) 1954.

LIST OF PRINCIPAL REFERENCES TO POEMS
INDIVIDUALLY DISCUSSED

(the arrangement is roughly chronological; the first titles being those of poems in *18 Poems*, the last belonging to poems in *Deaths and Entrances* and the new pieces in *Collected Poems*.)

Title	Page
I see the boys of summer	40–44
Where once the twilight locks no longer	44–46
A process in the weather of the heart	47
Where once the waters of your face	47
Before I knocked	47–49
My world is pyramid	49
From love's first fever to her plague	50
I dreamed my genesis	50
In the beginning	50–51
Especially when the October wind	51–55
If I were tickled by the rub of love	55–56
My hero bares his nerves	56–57
Our eunuch dreams	57–59
When, like a running grave	59
The force that through the green fuse drives the flower	59–61
All all and the dry world's lever	61–62
Light breaks where no sun shines	62–63
Was there a time	65
Should lanterns shine	65–66
Incarnate devil	66
Find meat on bones	67–68
The seed-at-zero	68–69
Altarwise by owl-light	69
I, in my intricate image	71–72
This bread I break	73–75
And death shall have no dominion	75–77

Title	Page
I have longed to move away	66–67, 77–78
Why east wind chills	78–80
Ears in the turret hear	80–81
The hand that signed the paper	81–82
How shall my animal	84
If my head hurt a hair's foot	85–86
After the funeral	86
Twenty-four years	88–89
The Conversation of Prayer	92–93
Vision and Prayer	94–96
A Refusal to Mourn the Death, by Fire, of a Child in London	96–98
Ceremony after a Fire Raid	98–99
A Winter's Tale	99–105
Poem in October	105–110
Fern Hill	110–113
The Hunchback in the Park	113–115
In my Craft or Sullen Art	115–116
Do not go gentle into that good night	116–118
Request for Leda	117
Ballad of the Long-legged Bait	118–119
Into her Lying Down Head	119–120
On the Marriage of a Virgin	120–121
On a Wedding Anniversary	121
Love in the Asylum	121–122
Unluckily for a Death	122–123
This Side of Truth	123–124
To Others than You	124–125
Deaths and Entrances	125
Holy Spring	125–126
Lie Still, Sleep Becalmed	126–127
When I Woke	127
Once below a time	127–128
In country sleep	130, 132–135
Over Sir John's hill	135–136
Poem on his birthday	136–138
Lament	138–140
In the white giant's thigh	140–142
Author's Prologue	142–143